Concepts and Careers in Physical Education

third edition

Robert D. Clayton
Joyce A. Clayton

Burgess Publishing Company
Minneapolis, Minnesota

Editorial: Wayne Schotanus, Nancy Crochiere, Anne Heller
Copy Editor: Gail Duke
Art Coordinator: Melinda Berndt
Cover design: Melinda Berndt
Composition: Gloria Otremba, K. F. Merrill Company

© 1982, 1977, 1972 by Burgess Publishing Company
Printed in the United States of America
Library of Congress Catalog Card Number 81-71145
ISBN 0-8087-2972-1

Burgess Publishing Company
7108 Ohms Lane
Minneapolis, Minnesota 55435

J I H G F E D C B A

Contents

iii

(1865-1900)—Athletics, Dancing, and Testing (1900-1930)—Reorientation and Fitness (1930-1960)—Lifetime Sports, Fitness, and an Academic Discipline (1960-Present)—Student Activities—Statements for Class Discussion—Bibliography

Chapter 5—The Foundations of American Physical Education   33

Introduction—Concepts to Be Gained From This Chapter—The Discipline of Physical Education—Is a Physical Educator a Teacher?—Definition of Physical Education—Discipline or Profession: What Difference Does It Make?—Definition of a Physical Educator—The Body of Knowledge in Physical Education—Preview of the Next Chapters—Your Aim—Student Activities—Statements for Class Discussion— Bibliography

Chapter 6—Physiological Foundations of Physical Education   43

Introduction—Concepts to Be Gained From This Chapter—Definition of Physiological Development—Historical Outline of Physiological Development—The President's Council on Physical Fitness and Sports— The Importance of Physiological Development— Education of the Physical—The Pendulum—Learning About Physiological Development— Physiological Development and You— Student Activities—Statements for Class Discussion— Bibliography

Chapter 7—Psychomotor Foundations of Physical Education   55

Introduction—Concepts to Be Gained From This Chapter—Definitions Related to Psychomotor Skills— Historical Outline of Psychomotor Learning—The Importance of Psychomotor Skills—The Learning Process— The Performance Process—Learning About Psychomotor Skills— Psychomotor Skills and You— Student Activities—Statements for Class Discussion— Bibliography

Chapter 8—Psychological Foundations of Physical Education   63

Introduction—Concepts to Be Gained From This Chapter—Definitions Related to Sport Psychology— Historical Background of Sport Psychology— The Value of Sport and Physical Activity to Psychosocial Development—

The Importance of Sport Psychology—Learning About Sport Psychology—
Sport Psychology and You—Student Activities—Statements for Class
Discussion—Bibliography

Chapter 9—Biomechanical Foundations of Physical Education   73

Introduction—Concepts to Be Gained From This Chapter—Definitions—
Historical Background of Biomechanics—The Importance of Biomechanics—
Learning About Biomechanics—Biomechanics and You—Student
Activities—Statements for Class Discussion— Bibliography

Chapter 10—Sociological Foundations of Physical Education   79

Introduction—Concepts to Be Gained From This Chapter—Definitions—
Historical Background of Sport—The Values of Sport—Sport in American
Life—Learning About Sport Sociology—Sport Sociology and You—Student
Activities—Statements for Class Discussion— Bibliography

CAREERS

Chapter 11—Careers in Physical Education   93

Introduction—Concepts to Be Gained From This Chapter—Societal
Trends—The Relationship of Physical Education to Health Education—The
Relationship of Physical Education to Recreation—Three Separate
Disciplines—Student Activities—Statements for Class Discussion—
Bibliography

Chapter 12—Teaching and Coaching   103

Introduction—Concepts to Be Gained From This Chapter—Basic Purposes of
Teaching Physical Education and Coaching Athletics—Physical Education
Teaching—Teaching in Schools—Teaching Overseas—Teaching Specialists—
The Researcher and Scholar—Coaching—Profile of Physical Education
Teachers and Coaches—Salaries of Physical Education Teachers and
Coaches—Job Satisfaction—Educational Preparation—Other Teaching
Areas—Student Activity—Statements for Class Discussion—Bibliography

Preface

This text is designed for students who are considering a career in physical education. While a few of you might understand the wide scope of physical education, most students are aware only of the teaching and coaching aspects. With these thoughts in mind, the purposes of these materials are:

1. To describe American physical education and the knowledges of science and society which contribute to this discipline
2. To discuss numerous career possibilities in physical education and to describe the characteristics and responsibilities of successful physical educators
3. To outline a program whereby your decisions concerning a possible role in physical education are influenced by appropriate career-education strategies.

If these purposes are reached, the ultimate goal is attainable—to have you make the correct decision as to whether you should (and could) continue the education necessary to become a successful physical educator.

This text is organized into four major areas: Commencement (Chapters 1-3), Concepts (Chapters 4-10), Careers (Chapters 11-15), and Commitment (Chapter 16). The Commencement section will alert you to effective strategies that will prove useful in determining if physical education is a suitable major. The Concepts chapters present background information on the physiological, psychological, biomechanical, psychomotor, and sociological foundations of our field. The Careers section contains material that describes a wide variety of sport and physical activity careers in the areas of sales, management, teaching, coaching, fitness, sports medicine, therapy and rehabilitation, performing, and sport media. Finally, the Commitment section calls for a decision concerning your future involvement in our field.

The evaluative tests (e.g., sport skills tests, teachers' personality inventory) that were included in the second edition of the book are now found in the instructor's guide. This allows the instructor greater flexibility in deciding when and how to administer the tests. The tests have been given to many prospective physical education majors and should enable you and your adviser to make a better decision on whether or not physical education is your logical career choice.

Acknowledgments

The third edition of this text has undergone numerous changes from the earlier ones. In the years between the initial thought of this project and its completion, many individuals have given their time and talent and should be thanked in print. Prof. William Bolonchuk, of the University of North Dakota, provided the impetus for the project by cooperating in the establishment of a skills testing program. Subsequently, Prof. Jean McCarthy, of Mankato (Minnesota) State University, provided additional help in this area, and also has reviewed critically several chapters in the earlier editions. Dr. Cindy Carlisle, of the University of Northern Colorado, and Dr. Barbara Aierstock, of Indiana University of Pennsylvania, have used the text in their Introduction to Physical Education classes and have provided valuable feedback.

Professional preparation is an ever-changing process. We hope that this text will enable students and professional educators alike to advance our discipline through understanding the concepts and processes that guide all of us toward meaningful careers in physical education.

Robert D. and Joyce A. Clayton

COMMENCEMENT

chapter 1

First Considerations

INTRODUCTION

Some students who read this text have just begun their college career and may be unfamiliar with some of the terms used to describe various aspects of this new environment and curious about the organization of the school. Regardless of your previous college experience, if you are reading this particular section, you are undoubtedly an undergraduate student; that is, you have not yet earned a Bachelor of Science or a Bachelor of Arts degree. Either of these degrees usually requires completing certain courses, earning satisfactory grades, and accumulating a certain number of credits. This process customarily takes four years. In the sections that follow, details of the process will be explained so that you can contribute when friends talk about general education, GPA, consent, the bulletin, the dean, and other such matters.

CONCEPTS TO BE GAINED FROM THIS CHAPTER

When you have mastered the material in this chapter, you will be able to demonstrate comprehension[1] of this concept:

---

[1]Your instructor will indicate the procedure by which you might demonstrate comprehension of this concept. It may be a written examination (short essay, multiple-choice, true-false, matching, or completion questions), a class discussion, a written composition, or other means. The standard of performance will also be established by the instructor.

A well-prepared person has extensive knowledge about a chosen school and a field of study. This will include information about:

1. Terms commonly used in colleges and universities
2. Rationale for general education courses
3. General education and physical education major (or minor) courses required at a particular school
4. Role of advisers
5. Organization of a particular school
6. Number of faculty members in the department (division)
7. Name of the chairperson of the department (division)

TERMS

Regardless of the area or subject, the student must understand certain common terms. The remainder of the text discusses many terms that relate specifically to physical education; this chapter will also discuss the specialized language of colleges and universities.

Prerequisites are requirements (courses or experiences) that must be satisfied before certain other courses may be taken. For example, algebra must usually be taken before trigonometry. It is quite common for *consent of the instructor* to be listed as the prerequisite, which indicates that, before enrolling in the course, you must get the instructor's permission. The primary practical problem about prerequisites is that students quite often overlook them! Should you fail to meet the prerequisites of a course and do not have the instructor's consent, you must then drop the course. This is usually costly and may cause a schedule problem.

Credits are numerical points given for each class taken; the number of credits is usually related to the number of formal hours spent in the class per week. Thus, a three-credit class meets three hours per week. Laboratory courses (i.e., nonclassroom courses) generally meet twice as often as classroom courses for the same number of credits. This implies that laboratory courses do not require as much time for outside study and thus do not merit the same credit as classroom courses. Physical education students, along with music and art students, customarily spend more time in actual class meetings than the credits indicate.

Ordinarily, grades are given for courses. In the majority of colleges, each grade is awarded *honor points* (A = 4, B = 3, C = 2, D = 1). Dividing a student's total credits into the honor points earned yields the *grade point average*, or *GPA*. For example, a student takes fifteen credits, earning ten credits of A and five credits of B: 10 credits × 4 = 40; 5 credits × 3 = 15. The student's GPA is 3.67 (55 ÷ 15). The GPA is probably the single most important record that you will accumulate in college. It is the common standard for comparing students and is checked by prospective employers and/or graduate schools. A recent trend is to permit some courses to be taken on a *credit-no credit* system. In such a case, a student who successfully passes the course receives credit but no letter grade. Students who are required to take a particular course and who are apprehensive about the final grade usually are pleased to use this option.

A school year is divided into *quarters* (from 10 to 11 weeks long) or *terms* or *semesters* (usually 15 to 16 weeks in length). Regardless of the system used, the length of time spent in the course determines the number of credits earned. An average load is 15 to 17 credits under either system, with 180 credits (quarter system) or 120 credits (semester system) being the usual minimum number required for graduation. When all requirements (credits earned, satisfactory GPA, required courses taken) are satisfied, a *degree* is awarded. The Associate in Arts degree may be earned after two years of study, while four years of study (perhaps including two at a community college) generally yields enough credits for the *bachelor's degree.*

Since course requirements, rules, and regulations change frequently, schools print an annual or biennial *catalog* or *bulletin.* Because of these changes, students usually have the option of meeting the requirements set forth for the year they enter college or for the year they plan to graduate. The college catalog or bulletin represents your contract with the school and obviously should be consulted at periodic intervals.

A term you will encounter early in college is *general education courses.* Sometimes called liberal education courses, they are required on the premise that part of a good education is to become more knowledgeable about the entire environment, as well as in a chosen field. Rightly or wrongly, these courses are sometimes unpopular with students.[2] General education courses normally account for about one-third of the total credits required for graduation. Sometimes these required courses are established by state law, but usually faculty and students have jointly cooperated in their formulation. The following list shows the common categories of general education courses, with a few specific examples of courses found in each:

> Communication skills—English, composition, speech, etc.
> Natural sciences—biology, chemistry, physics, etc.
> Humanities—philosophy, literature, music, art, etc.

There is a strong trend toward making general education more *elective,* which means that the student has some choice in course selection. For example, the general education requirement might read: "Select 12 credits from the Social Sciences." This gives you the option of selecting from whatever courses are considered part of the social sciences at your particular school (not all schools have the same combination of courses in each category). Since it is quite common to require general education courses as prerequisites to courses in the major, judicious selection may reduce the number of credits needed to meet all graduation requirements.

Other terms that must be understood relate to majors and minors. When a student has decided to do a great deal of college work in one particular area, with the thought that this concentration will be of value in later life (usually as a

---

[2]Faculty members hear complaints about general education courses. The following comment, written by a senior majoring in political science, is of interest: "Now I know that general education is a pain in the neck at times, and one asks himself, 'Why am I taking this stupid course?' The answer is that employers want a person with a broad liberal arts background. On the other side of the coin a person cannot be a businessman, nurse, etc. 24 hours a day. General education is designed to give you a well-rounded background in things that will probably help you enjoy other aspects of life also." (James Endres, letter to the editor, Mankato State University *Reporter,* Dec. 2, 1971, p. 3.)

vocation), the area chosen is known as the *major*. Many readers of this text are considering physical education as a possible major. If so, about 30 to 40 percent of the credits required for graduation will come from physical education and its related areas. For a *minor*, the chosen area is of secondary importance; it usually requires 15 to 20 percent of the credits for graduation. As there are many common requirements for either a major or a minor in physical education, you might begin taking it as a minor and then make it a major (or vice versa) with a minimum amount of program change. Depending upon your future plans, you may wish to secure a double major or two minors. The current bulletin of your school will give details of every program available.

At this point, it might be wise to acknowledge that students are often disappointed when they are not allowed to take a large number of courses in a major during their first year of college. You should realize that about one-half of all students change majors at least once in their college career. You will make a good start toward meeting general education requirements and obtaining a more realistic view of your chosen field by taking primarily general education courses and a sampling of courses in the proposed major.

An area of general concern is the selection of elective courses. Since the required credits in general education plus your major courses will seldom equal the total number required for graduation, you will have to elect additional courses. If you plan to teach, the state certification laws require that you take *professional education courses* (e.g., psychology of learning, growth and development of children, student teaching). These normally constitute 15 to 20 percent of the graduation credits. Should you be taking a nonteaching major, you may have a greater number of elective courses. It might be wise to select electives from one or two areas and thus complete one or two minors, rather than selecting only from courses recommended by classmates.

Finally, consider the role of *advisers*—the persons who serve as links between you and the school. The adviser can inform you of the latest curriculum changes and let you know when certain courses of importance are offered and can counsel you on problems related to school and to life in general. The primary duty of an adviser is to know you well enough to help you meet your educational objectives. Some students feel that they do not need an adviser—that they can graduate without such help. Some do graduate without help, but a surprisingly large number of students spend more time and money than needed merely because they failed to seek out their advisers or heed their advice.

ORGANIZATION OF THE COLLEGE OR UNIVERSITY

Because of the great number of possible majors and minors, colleges and universities are divided into various segments designed to meet the role assigned to them by society. The great diversity of size, location, financial resources, and personality of leaders means that no two colleges or universities are organized precisely alike. The major features of all schools are reasonably close to those shown in Figure 1.1.

The person in charge of the institution is the president (or chancellor). He or she has a group of advisers to aid in making top-level decisions; a Vice President for Academic Affairs (or Dean of Instruction) is designated as the person primarily

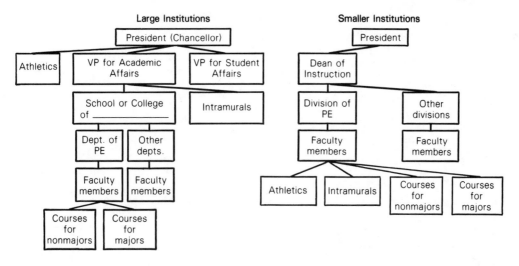

FIGURE 1.1. Typical organization of colleges and universities.

responsible for academic concerns. The typical college or university is organized into three to eight segments called schools, divisions, or sometimes colleges. Each represents a major area such as education, medicine, business, law, liberal arts, or industrial technology. In some institutions, physical education is one of these segments; the top person in each school, division, or college is usually a dean.

In institutions where these segments are responsible for several different areas (for example, the School of Education might include elementary and secondary education, special education, physical education, and counseling), one final subdivision is a department, usually led by a chairperson or department head. A group of faculty members composes the department in the area in which you intend to major. In theory, these individuals function as a team to carry out the aims of the department, the school or division, and the institution. Historically, many institutions have had separate physical education departments for women and for men. For various reasons, a recent trend has been to combine these departments.

Physical education departments in smaller schools usually include faculty members who specialize in athletics, intramurals, or teaching. In large schools, athletics (and sometimes intramurals) are completely separate from the physical education department.

Statements for Class Discussion

1. If you can pass a course without meeting the prerequisites, why worry about them?
2. If a student is not interested enough in physical education to major in it, he or she should seek another academic area, rather than minor in physical education.

chapter 2
Selecting Physical Education Students

INTRODUCTION

This text is usually read as students begin to study the academic discipline of physical education. The term "academic discipline" is probably new to you. Few people closely relate the word "academic" to physical education; in addition, to many people "discipline" implies punishment. No doubt you think of physical education as a particular class you took in high school. There it was considered a "subject," as were mathematics and English. At this particular moment, you must be thinking that working in physical education (probably teaching and/or coaching) is your goal. Perhaps it will be, but you should know more about physical education as an academic discipline and about your strengths and weaknesses in that area before you make a definite commitment. Likewise, most departments would like to know more about you before accepting you into their program. This chapter details the purposes of this text, provides definitions for such terms as "academic discipline" and "physical educator," and examines the rationale for a selection program. It begins with a listing of concepts that should guide you in your study.

CONCEPTS TO BE GAINED FROM THIS CHAPTER

When you have mastered the material in this chapter, you will be able to demonstrate comprehension of these concepts:

1. Because of its purposes, this text will be helpful both to the student and to the discipline of physical education.

2. Certain terms (physical education, physical educator, AAHPERD, screening test, selection program, self-selection, career education strategies) must be understood before one can intelligently discuss why and how prospective physical educators should be selected.
3. Regardless of selection devices, probably a combination of student self-selection and departmental screening is best.

PURPOSES OF THIS TEXT

This text is designed for students who are considering a career in physical education. While a few students may understand the wide scope of physical education, most are aware only of the teaching and coaching aspects. With these thoughts in mind, the purposes of these materials are:

1. To describe and to illustrate American physical education, the knowledges about science and society that contribute to this discipline, the career possibilities available to professionals, and the characteristics and responsibilities of successful physical educators.
2. To outline a program whereby your decisions concerning a future role in physical education are influenced by comparisons with current physical education majors and with successful professionals. These comparisons are reinforced by career-education strategies.

If these two purposes are reached, the ultimate goal is attainable—to have you make the correct decision as to whether you should (and could) continue the education necessary to become a successful physical educator.

WHAT IS PHYSICAL EDUCATION?

This chapter will make you aware of the procedures advocated by some colleges and universities as they select physical education students. You will be asked to judge the merit of these procedures. To do this most effectively, you should understand that physical education is more than a gym class, it is more than playing games, it is more than doing vigorous calisthenics. Physical education goes beyond coaching athletic teams and teaching people to dance. As a matter of fact, physical education does not always take place in the gym or on the playing field! Our definition, later amplified in Chapter 5, is that *physical education* is

1. An *academic discipline* that attempts to
2. *Investigate* the *uses* and *meanings* of
3. *Exercise, games, sports, athletics, aquatics, gymnastics,* and *dance*
4. To *understand* their *effects*
5. *On* and *for*
6. *Individuals* and *groups.*

In other words, physical education is the study of the many concepts and knowledges that relate to people and their movements.

WHAT IS A PHYSICAL EDUCATOR?

Characteristics of physical educators include being outgoing, being skilled in many sport activities, and being knowledgeable about the human body. All these characteristics contribute to the development of a stereotype—a mental picture of what people should be like if they are members of a particular group. The stereotype we would like you to visualize is a *person* who possesses such a

1. *Breadth* and *depth of knowledge*
2. Concerning at least *one key concept* of *human movement*
3. That he or she can function as a *scholar*, a *researcher*, and/or a *professional educator*.

At this point you are probably uncertain what we mean by a scholar or a researcher; you are probably more concerned with the absence of the terms "teacher" and "coach." A fuller discussion of this definition is given in Chapter 5.

TERMS RELATED TO SELECTION PROGRAMS

Before we can discuss the material in the remainder of this chapter, you must understand the following terms.

1. *AAHPERD*—American Alliance for Health, Physical Education, Recreation, and Dance. Members include college students who are preparing to work in health, physical education, recreation, or dance; teachers at all levels and other professional workers are also members.
2. *Screening test*—Some type of physical, mental, or social-emotional examination that aids a department in estimating how suited a person is for continuing education in the area of physical education. Quite often, a screening test is a shortened form of a longer test. An example is a basketball test consisting of field-goal shooting, dribbling, and passing, or a teacher aptitude test consisting of some of the questions from a longer test.
3. *Selection program*—The process for deciding which potential physical education majors have the desirable physical, mental, and social qualities that indicate that they will probably successfully complete their educational program.
4. *Self-selection program*—A process whereby you select your future career goal. The selection should be based upon awareness and exploration of possible career options, as well as knowledge of your interests and abilities.
5. *Career-education strategies*—Specific actions by you and/or the department which will enable you to make an appropriate career choice, at least for the present.

FACTORS THAT ENCOURAGE A DEPARTMENTAL SELECTION PROGRAM

Selection programs are widely used in such academic disciplines as medicine, law, and teacher training. It should be the responsibility of physical education departments to do likewise. The problem has always been, however, that no one admission test, no one personal interview, no one screening device is 100 percent accurate. But, faulty as selection programs might occasionally be, it must be remembered that in the long run they benefit both the student and the discipline.

First and foremost among the factors encouraging a selection process is the simple fact that there is a surplus of both men and women physical education teachers. Granted, there are careers other than teaching in which physical educators are needed, but not all physical education departments offer nonteaching options; those that do not should encourage the better-qualified students to remain and should make others aware of alternative career possibilities outside of physical education.

Second, departments know much more than they previously did about the physical skills and knowledge of successful physical education majors. Comparisons between your scores and others' will give the department some indication of your potential.

Third, the great influx of community college students has caused departments to lose one of their best means of selection—that of knowing a person for a period of one or two years. To some extent, a selection program enables faculty members to know students better.

Finally, maximizing learning is the aim of education. One way to achieve this is to permit students to waive courses or to earn credits by examination. Knowledge of a student's background, skills, and knowledge will help the school meet this aim.

COMPONENTS OF A SELECTION PROGRAM

Many departments in colleges and universities satisfy themselves in some way that the students majoring in their area do meet certain competence standards. Sometimes these standards are related only to grades received in high school courses, but often (as in foreign language, music, drama, art, or industrial science) students are expected to possess minimum performance skills as they begin their study. A selection program evaluates all students, selecting some and counseling others toward alternate careers.

For many years, AAHPERD has provided guidelines for professional preparation programs (AAHPERD 1948, p. 21; 1962, pp. 53, 69-70; 1974, pp. 24, 36). According to these sources, students should be assessed in at least these three areas: (1) ability to move effectively, (2) physical fitness level, and (3) physical skill in a number of sport activities. There is also widespread support for assessing a student's (4) ability to work successfully with persons of all ages. This criterion implies that a student's personality, leadership skills, and human relations aptitude are just as important as his or her motor skills.

Many departments have constructed their own screening tests, each structured somewhat differently. This difference is to be expected, as each department has a different view about levels and types of competence that are desirable and feasible in their particular situation. In this diversity, there is general agreement on two components of a selection program: (1) measurement of physical fitness and (2) measurement of skills in several commonly taught activities.

SELF-SELECTION PROGRAMS

While departmental selection programs may be regarded as desirable, research does not bear this out. For example, Nelson (1971) summarized a study at The Ohio State University. In 1964-65, first-year women majors at The Ohio State University were given a series of four physical tests and three scholastic aptitude tests. In 1970, the files of these former students were checked and separated into those who had graduated (N = 23) and the nongraduates (N = 80). The scores on each of the seven tests were checked and found to be of little value in predicting which students would "succeed" (graduate). Nelson concluded her report: "Perhaps the selection process lies in the informed choice of the student herself. Until more tests appear for this purpose, adequate advising, involvement in the department, early field experience, and the availability of academic and financial aid may make it possible for students to screen themselves by clarifying and acting upon their own goals" (Nelson 1971, p. 197).

We are convinced that physical fitness and physical skills are not the only attributes that should be evaluated and we are also convinced that it is not the responsibility of the physical education department alone to make the selection. Accordingly, Chapters 3 and 16 in this text describe suitable career-education strategies that will enable you to make a logical decision about your future in physical education. These strategies include a self-evaluation of your values and life style and an examination of your career goals. The tests in the instructor's guide make it possible to compare your scores on certain physical, mental, and psychological tests with the scores of other physical education majors and professionals in the field.

Thus, self-selection and departmental selection programs must be a cooperative endeavor. The more you know about the discipline of physical education and about yourself, the more certain you can be of your future career.

Student Activities

1. If your department has a selection program, list the requirements.
2. Not all schools have the facilities or the staff to conduct an effective selection program. If your school does not have such a program, interview one faculty member to find out the reasons.
3. Talk to other students who have transferred from community colleges or other four-year schools. Did their previous school have a selection program? If so, was it considered by the students to be reasonable and fair?

Statement for Class Discussion

Who should have the primary responsibility in the selection process—the department or the student?

Bibliography

AAHPERD. 1948. *Report of the National Conference on Undergraduate Professional Preparation in Health, Physical Education, and Recreation.* North Palm Beach, Fla.: Athletic Institute.
———. 1962. *Professional preparation in health education, physical education, and recreation education.* Reston, Va.: AAHPERD.

————. 1974. *Professional preparation in dance, physical education, recreation education, safety education, and school health education.* Reston, Va.: AAHPERD.

Brynteson, P. 1972. AAHPERD's number one priority should be standards. *JOPERD*[1] 43 (March): 32.

Nelson, B. 1971. Predicting success in the college physical education major program. *The Physical Educator* 28 (December): 196-197.

[1]Before January 1975, this journal was titled *JOHPER;* it was then retitled *JOPER.* In May 1981, its title was changed again, and it is now known as *JOPERD.* All references to the journal in this book will cite it as *JOPERD.*

chapter 3

Beginning Your Self-Selection Program

INTRODUCTION

Chapter 2 discussed selection programs; it concluded with the thought that perhaps two views—yours and the department's—might be desirable. The objective of this chapter is to outline how the remainder of this text can be used for your self-education. As you have noted, we indicate the concepts that you should gain after studying each chapter. Of more importance, however, is for you to become aware of your capabilities and interests in the psychomotor, cognitive, and affective domains related to physical education. This knowledge will enable both you and the department to make a more sound judgment as to your career potential in physical education.

This chapter begins with definitions of important terms. Then six desirable attributes of physical educators are discussed. Ways of evaluating each of the six—interest, physiological development, knowledge, motor skill development, personality, and attitude—are briefly described, and references to them in future chapters are noted. Finally, descriptions of various periodicals are given, so that you may begin to read about the many aspects of the discipline of physical education.

CONCEPTS TO BE GAINED FROM THIS CHAPTER

When you have mastered the material in this chapter, you will be able to demonstrate comprehension of these concepts:

1. Certain terms (the three educational domains, evaluation, motor skills, objective and subjective evaluation, raw scores) must be understood before a successful selection program can be undertaken.
2. A tentative evaluation of one's potential as a physical educator can be made as the reminder of this text is studied.
3. Reading scholarly, scientific, professional, and technical periodicals is essential to becoming a competent physical educator.

DEFINITION OF TERMS

Until a person understands the terms, it is difficult to speak the language! This is true in every branch of learning. Thus, the following terms should be studied before you proceed in this area.

1. *Domain*—As used in education, a general term that sets the boundaries of thought and study. For example, the "affective domain" relates to feelings, and not to knowledge of facts or the physical skill of hitting a ball. There are three educational domains, which will be discussed in this text—psychomotor, cognitive, and affective.
2. *Psychomotor domain*—Relates to the mind-body relationship that is present in virtually all physical movements. An example of a psychomotor skill is the ability to hit a pitched ball.
3. *Cognitive domain*—Includes the knowledge and understanding of facts, ideas, and thoughts that a person "knows" intellectually. The ability to answer a question correctly is primarily a cognitive skill.
4. *Affective domain*—Includes the feelings, attitudes, and values that a person possesses. Ideas about sportsmanship are examples of elements of the affective domain.
5. *Evaluation*—A procedure to ascertain how competent a person may be. Evaluation may be based on one or a number of factors tested in a variety of ways.
6. *Vocational interest inventory*—A test (usually written) in which a person indicates what types of things (jobs, leisure activities, hobbies) he or she would like to do. These answers are then matched against possible vocational choices.
7. *Motor skills test*—A test designed to measure the psychomotor skill ability of a person in a particular sport. It may be a sample of the activity or it may include every element of the activity.
8. *Objective evaluation*—The process of precisely determining the capacity, distance, speed, etc., of a student in a particular test item by using some type of measuring device. Timing the 100-yard dash with a stopwatch and counting the number of correct answers on a test are examples of objective measurements.
9. *Subjective evaluation*—The process of judging the skill of a person in a particular test item or entire activity. Watching a person run 100 yards and then classifying that person as efficient or competent in running ability would be a subjective judgment.

10. *Raw scores*—The actual (or first) result obtained in scoring a test. For example, when a student successfully makes 6 out of 10 free throws, the raw score would be 6. A score of 78 on a written test would be a raw score.

DESIRABLE ATTRIBUTES OF A PHYSICAL EDUCATOR

It would be easy to list desirable qualities (trustworthiness, loyalty, etc.) as necessary attributes of a good physical educator, but the same general list would apply to almost every role in life. However, there are at least six specific attributes that physical educators should possess. These are described below and then summarized in Table 3.1.

1. A most important attribute is *interest* in physical education as a career. All prospective majors say that they have a great interest in the field. Sometimes this interest is based on hero worship of the high school physical educator or coach. "I like to work with children" is often given as a reason, but the speaker may not realize that there are dozens of possible careers that involve working with children. You can evaluate your own interest in physical education in at least three ways:
   a. Taking, and having proper interpretation of, a *vocational interest inventory*. No doubt at some time in the past several years you have taken one of the many inventories that are available. If you haven't had such a test in the past year, however, it might be wise for you or your instructor to make arrangements with the counseling center of your school to do so. Remember that these tests are not absolute indicators; however, honest answers on your part will tell you where you are right now, and this is the first step in a meaningful self-evaluation.
   b. Reading and submitting reports on *articles* related to various chapters of this text. In the Bibliography at the end of each chapter, you will find a list of references that pertain closely to that topic. Perhaps your instructor will assign a certain number to read. Even if he or she does not, you can make a reasonably accurate subjective judgment about your interest in physical education by doing some reading in this area. If doing these readings seems like busywork, or you find you are putting them off until the last minute, your interest may not be as high as that of an enthusiastic, eager learner. (Another test is to see if you can read just one article in a periodical without finding two or three others of equal interest!)
   c. Participating in and reporting on a physical education field experience (school classes, Little League coaching, visiting a sporting goods store, etc.) that has a possible career attraction for you. Chapters 11-15 mention several possible places you might visit. Your instructor might ask you to gain actual experience in working with people in a situation of your choosing. This assignment should be both interesting and meaningful, if your interest in physical education is as high as it should be.

2. The attribute of *physiological development* is important for a physical education major. Chapter 6 discusses this as one of the cornerstones of American physical education.

3. *Motor skill development* is what most students think physical education is all about. How well you can perform the many activities that are a part of our program should be known as you begin your education, and your performance may be evaluated by psychomotor skills tests. These tests include skills that are part of the activity (in football, for example, passing for accuracy or punting for distance). Most serve as objective screening tests, although some are subjectively judged by an expert. Chapter 7 explains the rationale behind these motor skills tests. By using your raw scores, you can compare yourself with other prospective physical education majors.

4. *Knowledge* certainly is desired of prospective majors. This implies more than knowing the rules of an activity. There is a national knowledge test in physical education, based upon the physiological, psychological, sociological, and mechanical principles of movement. These principles are taught in a good school physical education program. Scales are available that will permit you to compare your score with others'. Chapter 9 describes the test more fully.

5. *Personality* is a key attribute in anyone's success. Counseling centers have the trained personnel to administer and interpret any of the several personality tests available. Unfortunately, the accuracy of such tests is open to question, and you should view the results of the tests only as a guide. Your instructor might permit this to be done in class; if not, then perhaps you can make an individual appointment with your school's counseling center for such an appraisal.

6. Finally, your *attitude* toward physical education as a career can be shown by the action you take after reading this text. Chapter 16 asks you to make a decision: Will you major in physical education? If so, this means taking the appropriate classes, joining professional groups, beginning to build your professional library, and participating in out-of-school professional activities. Specific advice that will help you prepare yourself for a successful career is outlined.

TABLE 3.1. ATTRIBUTES AND EVALUATIVE DEVICES NOTED IN THIS TEXT

ATTRIBUTES TO BE EVALUATED	EDUCATIONAL DOMAIN	EVALUATIVE DEVICES	LOCATION IN TEXT
1. Interest	Affective	1.a. Vocational interest inventory b. Read articles c. PE field experience	1.a. Chapter 3 b. Chapters 4–15 c. Chapters 12–15
2. Physiological development	Psychomotor	2.a. Youth fitness test b. Health-related fitness test	2. Chapter 6
3. Motor skill development	Psychomotor	3. Skills tests	3. Chapter 7
4. Personality	Affective	4. Personality tests	4. Chapter 8
5. Knowledge	Cognitive	5. Knowledge test	5. Chapter 9
6. Attitude	Affective	6. Essay	6. Chapter 16

PROFESSIONAL PUBLICATIONS

Table 3.2 presents a listing of publications devoted exclusively to topics of concern to physical educators. Many of these periodicals will be used at various times during the coming years; the sooner you become acquainted with them, the better!

TABLE 3.2. USEFUL PERIODICALS FOR PHYSICAL EDUCATORS

TYPE AND TITLE	CONTENT

SCHOLARLY
A. General Interest
   1. *Quest* (note: There are at least two magazines by this name; the one in physical education is published by NAPEHE).
   2. *Academy Papers* (of the American Academy of Physical Education)
	Scholarly articles related to philosophical, theoretical, or research questions basic to all aspects of human movement. Appeals primarily to college teachers in physical education.

B. Special Interest
   1. *Journal of Sport History*
   2. *Journal of the Philosophy of Sport*
	Specialized publications on theoretical and scholarly aspects of the particular topic. Intended for philosophers and historians as well as physical educators studying in these areas.

SCIENTIFIC
A. Physiological
   1. *Journal of Applied Physiology*
   2. *Journal of Physiology*
   3. *Journal of Sports Medicine and Physical Fitness*
   4. *Medicine and Science in Sports*
   5. *Physical Fitness/Sports*
   6. *Physical Fitness*
   7. *Research Quarterly for Exercise and Sport*
   8. *The Physician and Sportsmedicine*
	Articles that describe research results and/or practical applications. Aimed at physicians, exercise physiologists, athletic trainers, coaches, and teachers.

B. Biomechanical
   1. *Gymnast*
   2. *Journal of Biomechanics*
   3. *Journal of Sports Medicine*
   4. *Research Quarterly for Exercise and Sport*
	Mostly research-oriented articles, aimed primarily at experienced coaches and biomechanics researchers.

C. Psychological
   1. *International Journal of Sport Psychology*
   2. *Journal of Leisure Research*
   3. *Journal of Sport Psychology*
   4. *Research Quarterly for Exercise and Sport*
   5. *Review of Sport and Leisure*
	Scholarly reports of research or philosophical issues related to sport psychology.

D. Sociological
   1. *American Journal of Sociology*
   2. *International Review of Sport Sociology*
   3. *Journal of Leisure Research*
   4. *Journal of Sport and Social Issues*
   5. *Journal of Sport Behavior*
   6. *Research Quarterly for Exercise and Sport*
   7. *Review of Sport and Leisure*
	Articles written by and for sport sociologists and those studying in this area.

TABLE 3.2. (Continued)

TYPE AND TITLE	CONTENT

E. Psychomotor
  1. *Journal of Applied Psychology*
  2. *Journal of Motor Behavior*
  3. *Journal of Motor Learning*
  4. *International Journal of Physical Education*
  5. *Motor Skills: Theory into Practice*
  6. *Perceptual and Motor Skills*
  7. *Research Quarterly for Exercise and Sport*
	Articles that describe results of motor learning research and/or its practical application. Strategies for teaching are also discussed in these periodicals.

PROFESSIONAL
  A. Organizational Publications
    1. *Journal of Physical Education*
	Published by the YMCA monthly. General articles on HPERD.

2. *Journal of Physical Education, Recreation and Dance (JOPERD)*	Monthly publication of AAHPERD containing articles of interest to HPERD professionals and students.
3. *Update*	Monthly newspaper. Both *JOPERD* and *Update* are sent to student members of AAHPERD.

B. Fraternal publications
    1. *The Foil*
    2. *The Physical Educator*
	Published by Delta Psi Kappa (women's professional sorority) and Phi Epsilon Kappa (professional fraternity) respectively. Articles are related primarily to teaching or philosophical issues in physical education. The style of writing and the content appeal to student readers.

TECHNICAL
  A. Specialized Publications
    1. *Dance Magazine*
    2. *Runners' World*
    3. *Swimming Technique*
    4. *Track and Field News*
	Published by private companies or by organizations of coaches or teachers. Articles relate to the practical topics in each activity. There are many other such specialized magazines.

B. Coaching Publications
    1. *Athletic Journal*
    2. *Scholastic Coach*
    3. *Coaching: Women's Athletics*
	Published by private companies, these contain articles written by active coaches and/or researchers.

GENERAL INTEREST
  1. *Sporting News*
  2. *Sports Illustrated*
  3. *Women's Sports*
  4. *Sport*
	Published by private companies, these cover a wide sampling of information on sports in American society.

Student Activities

1. Search your school library to see which of the periodicals mentioned in this chapter are available. After locating them in the card catalog, actually find them on the shelves.
2. Find each of the following references in your school library; note how they might be useful to you later:
   a. *Reader's Guide to Periodical Literature*
   b. *Education Index*
   c. ERIC (Educational Resources Information Center)
   d. Microform Publications Bulletin

Statements for Class Discussion

1. The most important attribute of a beginning physical education major is _____.
2. The most important attribute of a professional physical educator is _____.
3. If physical education and athletics really improve a person's character (that is, honesty, sportsmanship, etc.), there should be very little vandalism in our section of the library.

Bibliography

Haag, E. 1979. Literature searching in physical education. *JOPERD* 50 (January): 54-58.

Owen, R. C. 1971. A record of physical education majors' participation in co-curricular and extra-curricular activities. *The Physical Educator* 28 (March): 27.

Sachs, M. 1979. Resources in sport sciences. *The Physical Educator* 34 (October): 119-121.

Turner, E. R., and Williams, H. P. 1973. Library vandalism and the physical education villains. *JOPERD* 44 (February): 39.

chapter **4**

A Brief History of American Physical Education

INTRODUCTION

In order to help you gain insight into the historical background of the subject, this chapter will summarize the highlights of five eras in physical education. You will discover that history has a way of repeating itself. The current emphasis on movement education is an outgrowth of the natural program advocated in the early 1900s. The participation by females in athletic competition in the 1970s had its genesis long before Title IX. The emphasis on physical fitness in 1960 was but another swing of the same pendulum. Knowledge of the past can help in understanding the present and in forecasting the future.

Historical material, as presented in this chapter, probably seems related only to the cognitive domain—that is, it provides facts and dates by which we gain knowledge. Actually, we hope that the affective domain is also included, because an appreciation of history influences the shaping of our views and philosophies. Historical facts must be synthesized into current knowledge and situations; only then can the best possible decisions be made.

CONCEPTS TO BE GAINED FROM THIS CHAPTER

When you have mastered the material in this chapter, you will be able to demonstrate comprehension of these concepts:

1. Play, games, dance, and sport (collectively called physical education) have been a part of American life since 1620.
2. To remain essential to American education, physical education has had to change with the times. Thus, changes have occurred in:
   a. The objectives of the program
   b. The activities taught, supervised, and coached
   c. The professional preparation of physical educators
   d. Emphasis on physical fitness, both school age and adult
   e. The role of athletics in the schools
   f. Participation by girls and women in athletics
   g. Participation by the public in sport and physical activity.

RECREATION, GYMNASTICS, AND CALISTHENICS (1620-1865)

The beginnings of physical education in the United States were modest and informal. Although various European nations (especially Germany, Sweden, and Denmark) had evolved specific programs geared to their needs, no one system of physical education came to this country with the colonists. In early colonial days, New England was the only section of the country without games; this is usually attributed to the strict Puritan beliefs held at that time. The Dutch (in New York) and the English (in Virginia) encouraged recreational activities of a physical nature, although there was no organized movement as such. Because the aim of education was popularly considered to be the "3 Rs," the few schools that were established provided no place for physical education or recreation. The first record of any school encouraging sports for recreation's sake was Samuel Moody's Summer School in Massachusetts, begun in 1763.

When the academies began to appear in the Eastern seaboard states in the early nineteenth century, scholastic physical education appeared in the curriculum. The founders of these institutions believed that good health was a prerequisite for a good life, that a person should be able to participate in sports, and that shorter school hours provided ample time for sports. These reasons, along with the influence of prominent European leaders who favored a planned physical education program in schools, led to the inclusion of physical activities in the daily life of students. Because physical education came after school, these private institutions did not attempt to control this activity; instead, it was left to student organization.

Immigrants and immigration were responsible for the ultimate inauguration of physical education in the public schools. When the Round Hill School in Massachusetts was established in 1825, the founders believed so strongly in physical training that they hired a German gymnastics instructor named Beck to supervise the students in this activity. Beck was the forerunner of the early foreign instructors, who worked primarily in the Northeast. However, the primary impetus in the field of physical education was a result of the great immigration of Germans to this country. Because they spoke little or no English, they tended to live together in cities and to establish their own societies. The most prominent of these societies was the United Turnverein of North America. Although this movement had three aims (intellectual enlightenment, sociability, and physical development), the latter aim seemed to be most important. Prior to the Civil War, membership in this organization numbered 10,000, and a training school for leaders was established. (There are "Turner" groups active in certain cities and towns of the United States today. In most cases, they are noted for their outstanding gymnastic programs.)

A growing belief in the value of physical activity led to the passage of a law in Boston in 1853; it stated that all children in elementary school must have a daily period of physical exercise. Because teachers were not trained to lead the activity, however, this rule was not enforced. In 1855, the City of St. Louis reported that some physical education was taking place in its schools. Because gymnastics was a regular part of the curriculum in many European countries, it was only natural that immigrants to the United States brought pressure upon local school boards to include it in the school curriculum.

During the Civil War (as has happened during subsequent periods of war in the United States), the physical weakness of American youth was cited as a main reason for the inclusion of physical education in the school curriculum of every city and town. Although this argument was primarily directed to boys, other persons were advocating increased physical training for women at this time. Dio Lewis argued that German gymnastics discriminated against age and sex and that only his system (as taught in his Normal Institute for Physical Education in Boston) would properly develop both boys and girls. While he was unpopular with others in the field, it must be noted that he was the motivating force behind the adoption of physical education in school curricula during the period 1860-1865.

Through the years, many outstanding women leaders in the field have made significant contributions. The forerunner was Catherine Beecher who, as early as 1828, advocated physical education for women. She founded two private girls' schools, and is considered to be the first native-born American to formulate a comprehensive gymnastic system adapted to American needs. Although no particular movement can be credited to her, she is to be remembered as the earliest proponent of and crusader for physical education for women in the United States.

GYMNASTICS AND MEASUREMENT (1865-1900)

The period 1865-1900 in America can generally be termed one of "education for nationalism." The heavy immigration, the westward movement, the growth of centralized government, and the industrial development of the country all combined to ensure that the American life style would change. Education underwent profound changes—widespread free schooling, the idea of compulsory education, tax-supported high schools, expanded curriculum in natural and social sciences, child labor laws, and the idea of social education as a proper aspect of the curriculum. The aims of education included the broadening of the scope of training, the inculcation of social ideals, and an emphasis on vocational subjects in high school. The aims of physical education were hygienic, educative, and remedial.

After the Civil War, a battle of a different type (but of almost equal vigor) developed among professional workers over the relative merits of the Swedish gymnastic system versus the German system. "The Swedish system was supposed to have a scientific basis in studies of human anatomy, whereas the German gymnastics had been a more spontaneous movement" (Nixon and Cozens 1947, p. 31). Actual debates on the subject were held, with neither side conceding. School administrators were in the middle of this issue, since their physical education specialists were usually trained in only one system. Eventually, it became common to see apparatus of both systems in school gymnasiums.

While the argument between advocates of the German and Swedish systems raged, other issues were being considered. During the Civil War, military training had almost exclusively replaced physical education in colleges and universities. This trend spread to high schools and was continued in some cases long after the end of the war.

In 1889, a physical training conference was held in Boston, which was to have great influence upon the program of physical education for many years. At this meeting, the educators in attendance proposed a number of conditions that were to be met by a physical education program if it were to be incorporated as a part of the regular school curriculum. In effect, they stated that such a program must require very little time, must be inexpensive, must not demand specially trained teachers, must take place in the classroom (because activity outside the classroom was assumed to be noneducative), and must not require apparatus. This was accepted by physical educators at that time, and—although we no longer believe that education occurs only in the classroom—the idea of "10 minutes per day of calisthenics taught by the classroom teacher (grades K-6)" still hinders the effectiveness of programs in some localities.

An important development for later physical education occurred during this period, which may be termed "tests and measurements." Although the specific techniques may no longer be used, the concept that scientific tools and procedures should be employed in physical education remains. Anthropometric measurements and strength testing were given to thousands of students from elementary level through college during the years 1885-1900.

During this period, there was no relationship between athletics and physical education at either the college or high school level; athletics took place after school and were semiorganized. The prevailing attitude toward athletics in public schools was that they were unnecessary, since most children had chores that consumed their excess time and energy.

A great influence on the curriculum in physical education was the preparation of teachers. Mention has already been made of Dio Lewis' school in Boston and the Normal Schools of the Turnverein movement. Several private schools were founded during this period; the most notable were Sargent's school in Cambridge, Anderson's school in New Haven, the YMCA in Springfield, Mass., and the Boston Normal School of Gymnastics. All of these schools had different training procedures and curricula. Eventually, the students seemed to develop an appreciation for other schools and systems; thus, by 1900, the bitterness that marked earlier years had largely disappeared.

Another development that was to have a great influence on curricula in later years was the organization of various professional groups. In 1885, the forerunner of the American Alliance for Health, Physical Education, Recreation, and Dance was formed. This group (AAHPERD) is now regarded as the national voice for all physical educators.

State legislation, making physical education compulsory, was initiated in 1892 in Ohio. Facts regarding the exact dates of the passage of such legislation in the older states are inconsistent among several sources; it is known, however, that Ohio, California, North Dakota, Wisconsin, and Idaho were among the earliest states to pass compulsory physical education laws. The forces behind these laws included interest groups in the various states: the Turnverein, the Women's Christian Temperance Union (WCTU), and various professional teacher organizations.

Although the number of professionally trained workers in physical education was small during this era, at least four are regarded as true pioneers. Dr. Edward Hitchcock of Amherst College conducted the only organized college program of physical education up to 1865. All students took his classes, which were aimed at hygienic and recreational purposes. He was a medical doctor and the first physical educator to be appointed as a full faculty member in an American college. His primary interest was anthropometry. Dr. Dudley Sargent, another medical doctor, established what was termed the "Sargent system" of physical education. This was actually a combination of Swedish and German gymnastics, plus sports, athletics, and measurement. His two distinctive contributions were in the field of teacher training and in the invention of numerous exercise devices that the user could adapt to personal strength. W. G. Anderson, M.D., the instigator of the American Alliance for Health, Physical Education, Recreation, and Dance, was influential in teacher preparation. Amy Morris Homans was originally drawn into teacher training because of a strong conviction about the need for trained women teachers. She became head of the physical education department at Wellesley College and exerted profound influence on teacher training.

ATHLETICS, DANCING, AND TESTING (1900-1930)

The three decades between 1900 and 1930 saw the United States enter a world war, rise to unprecedented economic heights, and then plunge into a great depression. The physical education movement was vitally affected by each of these major developments. It was also affected by the scientific, developmental, and social education movements that then began to assume prominence. The social education movement was the most influential, promulgating the idea that the school should be a miniature society with a flexible curriculum.

Physical education was gradually moving from the foreign systems of gymnastics toward what was called the "New Physical Education." In 1910, Clark Hetherington defined the four phases of the educational process for the new physical education as follows:

1. *Organic education*—A process to develop vigor. This refers to nutrition and elimination as well as to physical development.
2. *Psychomotor education*—The process that develops power and skill in neuromuscular activities.
3. *Character education*—The development of moral, social, and spiritual powers.
4. *Intellectual education*—The child learns by doing, especially through play.

The profession faced increased challenges from several directions. With the new century came a determined effort to bring athletics and dancing into the physical education curriculum as an acknowledged part of education, not merely as something for school children to organize and to conduct for themselves after school hours. This presented a challenge to the gymnastics devotees to protect their heretofore unquestioned monopoly of the program. The "battle of the systems" now gave way to a new conflict of gymnastics versus dancing and athletics (Lee and Bennett 1960, p. 39).

By 1920, the athletic movement—and the playground movement, which also arose at that time—were indications that professional workers were revolting against formalism in educational training. As the athletic movement and the recreation movement began to capture the immediate interests of youth, gymnastics started to lose favor. The games that were being played after school began to be taught as a part of the regular physical education program. Although the new program appeared to be an improvement over the formal gymnastic system, the fact was that the pendulum began to swing too far, and professional workers began again to divide into opposing camps. Williams (1949, p. 177) reported on that state of confusion:

> Thus, for more than three decades after 1889, examples of the two types of physical education in the school could be found; one, composed of artificial exercises, arose in response to a group of ideas wholly foreign to the traits, characteristics, and needs of American boys and girls and which were justified by those who proposed them on the grounds of correction of defects, acquirement of health or promotion of discipline. . . . The other was represented by the extreme development of competitive athletics which arose as a natural activity of youth, stimulated by the commercial and advertising values of games and without the educational leadership which such an activity should attract.

The entry of the United States into World War I meant that the usual wartime programs of fitness replaced the traditional program. While this was advantageous in that it permitted a change to a new program after the war, it certainly did not help professional workers conduct the most efficacious program for all concerned.

Measurement in physical education, as we understand it today, dates from 1920. Strength testing declined during this era, while athletic achievement tests, classification tests, cardiovascular tests, motor ability tests, and character-rating tests all began their development from crude methods to refined tools useful to the discipline.

The leaders of this period were Luther Gulick, James McCurdy, Thomas Wood, and Clark Hetherington. Gulick and McCurdy, both associated with the YMCA college in Springfield, Mass., were the links between the older "gymnastics" and the "New Physical Education" of the future. They were scholars as well as teachers and served as the acknowledged leaders of the profession during this time. Wood and Hetherington were philosophers, in the sense that they visualized a purpose for physical education beyond the prevailing view of the subject as mere "perspiration and muscle building." Wood began his opposition to all foreign gymnastics systems around the turn of the century, while Hetherington's influence began in 1913.

REORIENTATION AND FITNESS (1930-1960)

The continuing years of the Depression brought about an increased unwillingness to include physical education in the curriculum of the public schools. Fortunately, because of the tremendous support given by AAHPERD, physical education remained very much a part of the school curriculum.

During the years 1930-1941, physical education continued to change more in theory than in actual practice. Although there was less emphasis upon gymnastics, the general economic situation prevented schools from securing additional equipment or facilities to keep up with the latest philosophical thinking. An oversupply of physical education teachers enabled schools to select better personnel. The fact that many states sharply upgraded educational requirements for teachers meant that those who followed current philosophies of physical education were usually selected as replacements for traditionally trained teachers. Van Dalen, Mitchell, and Bennett (1953, p. 472) reported that in 1930 few states required more than one year of training for physical educators; by 1940, all but a few required two to four years of training.

The aims of physical education continued to be modified during this era. The philosophies of Wood and Hetherington were adapted by Williams and Nash, both of whom went beyond the old concept of gymnastics for the development of strength and vigor. A new aim, preparation for leisure time, was advocated and readily accepted, especially since the economic hardships of the period created enforced leisure time for many. The value of active participation in athletics (for boys) was stressed, but not for the same reasons as earlier; the adjustments that students had to make in social situations were now thought to be more important than their moral development. Athletic participation for girls and women was advocated by very few citizens and by even fewer women physical educators. In fact, Mrs. Herbert Hoover's assertion that athletic competition was unladylike was so influential that female athletes had less opportunities than before. During World War II, physical fitness was stressed, but this was also the first wartime period when there was no large substitution of military training for physical education.

The scope of the physical education curriculum broadened considerably during this era. Calisthenics, rhythmic movements, apparatus work, tumbling, athletic contests, team games, swimming, mass games, dance, tennis, golf, handball were all properly included in the program. Because the emphasis had shifted from the word "physical" to the word "education," any activity that properly provided for this function could be included. Most high schools had a wide variety; it was common to find 15 different activities offered to students during their high school years. A great many school systems continued to emphasize boys' sports, however, even if it meant offering fewer activities. By state law, schools had to offer physical education classes, but many times these were little more than free-play sessions.

A report on the low physical fitness level of American children, published in 1953, signaled the beginning of a return to one of the original aims of physical education. Although usually not considered a valid fitness test by most experts, the Kraus-Weber Test provided the impetus for President Eisenhower's creation of the President's Council on Youth Fitness. Ironically, AAHPERD was not invited to attend; participants were national sport figures and physicians. Eventually, AAH-PERD was asked to devise a national fitness test; this was done in 1957.

To recount the influences of all the prominent persons in physical education for this period of time would be a monumental task. J. F. Williams and J. B. Nash have been mentioned earlier as proponents of differing aims of physical education; Williams especially was responsible for the greatly increased emphasis on social and carryover values. In the area of philosophy and objectives of physical education, the writings of C. H. McCloy and Delbert Oberteuffer were studied. In the development of intramurals, Elmer D. Mitchell was supreme. C. H. McCloy, T. K. Cureton, and Peter Karpovich were regarded as leaders in scientific measurement.

LIFETIME SPORTS, FITNESS, AND AN ACADEMIC DISCIPLINE (1960-Present)

Continuing the emphasis upon fitness, in 1963, President Kennedy changed the name and aim of Eisenhower's council to the President's Council on Physical Fitness. Millions of Americans of all ages were tested with the Youth Fitness Test, and thousands earned one of the various awards offered by the council. This test was given to both American and foreign students; comparisons on this basis were usually unflattering to Americans! Fitness became more evident in girls' programs, but still received less emphasis than it did in boys' programs. Several adult physical fitness programs achieved popularity, beginning with the Canadian Air Force 5BX Program and continuing with jogging, aerobics, and cycling. Much advertising time and space were donated to the fitness cause.

The Lifetime Sports Foundation became operative in the mid-1960s. This group was composed of sporting goods companies and sporting groups (such as the National Bowling Proprietors Association). They each contributed money both to print materials that would help teachers do a better job in training people in certain lifetime sports (bowling, golf, archery, tennis) and to conduct workshops in which teachers could actually participate in a training program conducted by a master teacher.

Athletics was attacked and supported with equal vigor by many groups. The taxpayers' reluctance to support school-bond issues caused some school boards to curtail or to suspend athletic competition. Certain national authorities, including prominent physical educators, called for a "new" athletic program that would eliminate what they considered overemphasis on a few major sports. On the other hand, the demand for high school coaches grew so great that special coaching certificates were offered by many colleges. There was an increase in the number of junior varsity teams sponsored by schools in a wider variety of sports (such as gymnastics, ice hockey, bowling, and skiing) so that more students might become participants.

The increase in sport teams in the 1970s was unique in that athletic opportunities for girls and women doubled and tripled in many schools. Before this time women physical educators had advocated "play days" rather than interschool competitions. The "new" physical educators felt that athletics could be as beneficial to girls as to boys, so they began to request "equality of opportunity."

Overall, sport in schools, as measured by student participation, grew greatly during this period, even though a number of men's teams sponsored by athletic departments were eliminated because of financial woes. Title IX of the Higher Education Act became effective in July 1975; this resulted in the allocation of much more money for girls' and women's sports. Colleges were especially hard pressed to provide the equity that Title IX mandated. The Association of Intercollegiate Athletics for Women (AIAW), similar to the National Collegiate Athletic Association (NCAA), which for years had sponsored men's athletic championships, became the governing body for collegiate women's sports. The National Association of Intercollegiate Athletics (NAIA), composed of small colleges, had already promoted women's championships. In 1981, the NCAA proposed sponsorship of women's championships, which was met with vigorous dissent from the AIAW. Fierce rivalry and questionable strategy were not confined to the playing fields!

The boom in athletics also extended downward. Little League baseball, Pop Warner football, Biddy basketball, and age-group track and swimming are examples of flourishing sports programs for boys and girls.

Professional sports also enjoyed an ever-increasing public acceptance beginning in the early 1960s. Teams were moved from city to city, new leagues (soccer, indoor soccer, tennis) were formed, and the number of teams in established sports such as football, basketball, and ice hockey expanded. Television revenue, the chief impetus behind the astronomical salaries paid to superstars, became a dominant force in scheduling contests. Cable and pay TV, which many predict will eventually be in common use throughout the United States, also began to influence both college and professional sports.

Public participation in lifetime sports continued to climb. The reduction in the work week, three-day national holidays, and increased amounts of spending money all contributed to an annual increase of public involvement in physical activity. Swimming became the favorite adult fitness activity of the 1980s, even as joggers were being banned from the streets of one California city as a traffic hazard. Physicians specializing in sport injuries had many adults among their patients. Thousands of people ran in marathons; many more bought warmup suits costing over $75. Every sign pointed to public acceptance of physical activity. A 1979 Gallup poll found that 76 percent of Americans felt that physical education was an essential school subject—and adults apparently felt that activity was good for them, too.

Up to this point, the historical facts mentioned have all related to the practical application of physical education to the well-being of society. The early emphasis on health as a goal, then games, athletics, and dancing, then leisure activities, then back to fitness—all of these are professional in nature. Until 1964, little attention was given to the relationship of physical education to other disciplines. It was at this time that physical educators began to initiate the research and reflective thinking that characterize an academic discipline. The American College of Sports Medicine attempted to motivate physicians, health educators, and physical educators into becoming more aware of the interrelationship between medicine and the health sciences.

Project ACE (Alliance Career Education), funded by the federal government in 1979-1980, was the beginning of a concerted effort by AAHPERD to develop other physical education careers besides teaching. Students were encouraged to become aware of specific opportunities in sport performance, communication, sales, management, fitness, rehabilitation, and therapy. It is to be hoped that students will turn an interest in sport and physical activity into meaningful and needed careers.

Groups of sport scholars and researchers in psychology, psychomotor learning, sociology, history, philosophy, pedagogy (teaching), and biomechanics were also formed. All these groups served to focus attention on physical education as an academic discipline as well as a profession.

Student Activities

1. Many colleges and universities offer master's degrees and doctorates. One of the requirements for either degree is a research project called a thesis or a dissertation. Look in the library card catalog under "Physical Education—History" for any thesis or dissertation that was written at your school. Read any one.
2. Examine related periodicals (history, sociology, etc.) for articles about early physical education. Read one or more.
3. There are several recent books on physical education history. Determine which of these are available in your library and read a chapter in any one.
4. If you are taking English, history, economics, sociology, or political science, and a term paper is required, consider as a topic some aspect of physical education. Possibilities: Physical Fitness, The Importance of Sport in the United States, Spectator Problems at Athletic Events, Fitness Fads, Charles Atlas: A Physical Educator?, Title IX and Its Implications for Sport, Is Fishing a Part of Physical Education?

Statements for Class Discussion

1. The aim of physical education in school is to have fun.
2. There are valid reasons for an increase in women's participation in athletics.
3. Some early physical education movements contributed significantly to today's physical education philosophy; others detracted from it.
4. The separate development of physical education and athletics in early times has contributed to today's separation of these two programs in many schools.

Bibliography

Bennett, B. L. 1970. Curious relationship of religion and physical education. *JOPERD* 40 (September): 69.
Boyle, R. H. 1955. The report that shocked the President. *Sports Illustrated* 3 (August 15): 38.
———. 1962. The bizarre history of American sports. *Sports Illustrated* 16 (January 8): 54-62.
Cantwell, R. 1975. America is formed for happiness. *Sports Illustrated* 43 (December 19): 54-71.
Coursey, L. 1980. Pioneer black physical educators. *JOPERD* 51 (May): 54-56.

Gerber, E., *et al.* 1974. *The American woman in sport.* Reading, Mass.: Addison Wesley Co.

Gerber, E. W. 1972. Early professional preparation curriculum in the United States. *The Physical Educator* 29 (March): 38.

Hayes, E. 1980. Development of dance in the Alliance from the beginnings of dance education in universities to the "D" in AAHPERD. *JOPERD* 51 (May): 32-36.

Hetherington, C. 1910. Fundamental education. *Proceedings and Addresses, National Education Association:* 350-377.

Kennedy, R. 1979. Oh, what an era! *Sports Illustrated* 47 (August 13): 52-60.

Kroll, W., and Lewis, G. 1969. The first academic degree in physical education. *JOPERD* 40 (June): 73-74.

Langston, D. 1968. Sports on stamps. *JOPERD* 39 (May): 38-39.

Lee, M., and Bennett, B. 1960. This is our heritage. *JOPERD* 31 (April): 25-85.

————. 1972. John Richard Betts and the beginning of a new age in sports history. *JOPERD* 43 (March): 81.

Little, J. R. 1970. Charles Harold McCloy: Ten years hence. *The Physical Educator* 27 (May): 57.

Massengale, J. D. 1979. The Americanization of school sports: Historical and social consequences. *The Physical Educator* 36 (May): 59-69.

Mealy, R. 1972. The "battle of the systems." *The Physical Educator* 29 (May): 66-69.

Nixon, E. W., and Cozens, F. W. 1947. *An introduction to physical education.* Philadelphia: W. B. Saunders Co.

Park, R. J. 1969. The philosophy of John Dewey and physical education. *The Physical Educator* 26 (March): 55.

Parker, F. 1970. Sport, play and physical education in cultural perspective. *JOPERD* 41 (January): 29-30.

Redmond, G. 1973. A plethora of shrines: Sport in the Museum and Hall of Fame. *Quest* 19 (January): 41-48.

Sargent, D. A. 1906. *Physical education.* Boston: Ginn and Co.

Spears, B. 1971. "Building up character has been my aim": A glimpse of the life of Mary Hemenway. *JOPERD* 42 (March): 93.

Twenter, C. J. 1972. History speaks, but who listens? *The Physical Educator* 29 (May): 89.

Van Dalen, D. B., Mitchell, E. D., and Bennett, B. L. 1953. *A world history of physical education.* Englewood Cliffs, N.J.: Prentice-Hall.

Vanderzwaag, H. 1970. Sports concepts. *JOPERD* 41 (March): 35-36.

Welch, J. E. 1967. The impact of Edward Hitchcock on the history of physical education. *The Physical Educator* 24 (May): 54-56.

————. 1973. Edward Hitchcock and the early years of AAHPER. *JOPERD* 44 (February): 50-54.

Williams, J. F. 1949. *The principles of physical education.* Philadelphia: W. B. Saunders Co.

Wilson, C. 1969. They had a dream. *The Physical Educator* 26 (December): 173.

chapter 5

The Foundations of American Physical Education

INTRODUCTION

This chapter will outline the reasons for describing physical education as an academic discipline, the relationship of a profession to a discipline, and the body of knowledge that constitutes physical education. This chapter serves as a guide to Chapters 6-10, which discuss in detail each of the five major areas in the body of knowledge that physical educators must study.

CONCEPTS TO BE GAINED FROM THIS CHAPTER

When you have mastered the material in this chapter, you will be able to demonstrate comprehension of these concepts:

1. Physical education meets the two accepted criteria of a discipline.
2. After adequate education, physical educators may become scholars, researchers, and/or professional educators.
3. Because of their specialized and narrow education, some persons become technicians rather than scholars, researchers, and/or professional educators.

THE DISCIPLINE OF PHYSICAL EDUCATION

The term "physical education" is thought by many to be an inaccurate description of our field. "Physical" implies that the mind and body can be divided, while "education" seems to imply that we are concerned primarily with some branch of teaching. There is no doubt that the public considers physical education as a school subject, that athletics and physical education are synonymous terms, that homework is seldom required to pass our courses, and that playing games is our trademark. Although there is some truth to these observations, it is also true that what we study, investigate, and teach in this field covers a much broader area than is generally believed.

In a very influential article, Henry (1964, p. 7) says that an academic discipline may be characterized by two major criteria:

1. It is an organized body of knowledge collectively embraced in a formal course of study.
2. The acquisition of such knowledge is assumed to be an adequate and worthy objective, without any demonstration or requirement of practical application.

We contend that physical education does meet these two criteria. An educated person should know a number of facts, concepts, ideas, and hypotheses. These include more than merely knowing how to play volleyball or knowing the rules of ice hockey. They deal with physiological development, how learning to move efficiently affects mental learning, and when it is appropriate to build new facilities so that more people can participate. In short, physical education is a formal course of study utilizing the sport perspectives of biomechanics, exercise physiology, sociology, psychology, history, medicine, and philosophy (Rivenes 1978).

Rarick (1967, pp. 51-52) expands upon Henry's comments by illustrating some of the areas that are part of our body of knowledge. According to Rarick:

1. Physical education as a discipline is concerned with the mechanics of human movement, with the mode of acquisition and control of movement patterns, and with the psychological factors affecting movement responses.
2. Physical education is concerned with the physiology of people under the stresses of exercise, sports, and dance and with the immediate and lasting effects of physical activity.
3. The historical and cultural aspects of physical education and dance occupy a prominent place in our discipline. The roles of sports and dance in the cultures that have preceded ours and in our own culture need to be fully explored.
4. Lastly, in physical education we are aware that people do not function alone. Individual and group interactions during games, sports, and dance are an important area, one that needs our attention.

As you might expect, not all physical educators agree precisely on the fundamental position that physical education is a discipline. Ulrich and Nixon (1972, pp. 11-13) maintain that physical education is a subdiscipline of the discipline of human movement; they depict it as shown in Figure 5.1.

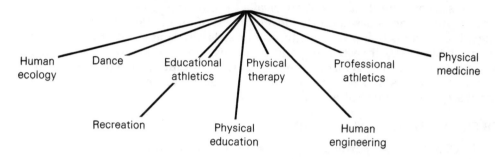

Figure 5.1. The discipline of human movement phenomena contains at least these nine subdisciplines. Adapted from C. Ulrich and J. Nixon, *Tones of theory* (Reston, Va.. AAHPERD, 1972), p. 12. Used by permission.

Whether we are a discipline or subdiscipline is really not as important as whether or not we "know where we are going." All physical educators agree that the interaction of people and their movements is our primary area of interest; we cannot merely borrow facts and ideas from existing disciplines. We must support our own discipline through an organized program of study, research, and professional activity.

IS A PHYSICAL EDUCATOR A TEACHER?

For years, physical educators have considered themselves members of the teaching profession. But such activity is just part of our focus. Rivenes (1978, p. 8) points out that:

> A discipline describes, explains, and predicts phenomena related to a subject matter; it develops a body of knowledge. A profession, on the other hand, tries to improve the conditions of society through some kind of service. A discipline seeks to understand a subject matter, a profession to implement change. A profession is based on a discipline in that professional programs and practices develop in accordance with known facts.

Henry's second criterion indicates that a discipline might not have practical application, and it is on this point that a decided change of opinion has occurred within the ranks of physical educators. The "practical application" test influenced all professional preparation; the feeling was that if it did not relate to teaching, it was not really appropriate to physical education. Now, many departments are recognizing that physical education majors may do things other than teach. This new development will make the discipline much more respected and useful.

Thus, a competent teacher of physical education is a professional educator. But since a profession is based on the development of an intellectual body of knowledge, it is obvious that physical education needs different types of workers. Some spend their careers investigating and reporting the results of theoretical, idealistic, and scientific inquiry, while others deal with the application of these results as a service to others. The teaching of physical education is one specialized career in the discipline of physical education.

DEFINITION OF PHYSICAL EDUCATION

In Chapter 2, we defined physical education as follows:

> Physical education is an academic discipline that attempts to investigate the uses and meanings of exercise, games, sports, athletics, aquatics, gymnastics, and dance to understand their effects on and for individuals and groups.

Most of the older definitions (formulated before 1965) indicate only that physical education is the guidance of a person's physical activity, with the goal of helping the person develop desirable physical, social, emotional, and intellectual traits. The new definition suggests that guidance of physical activity (e.g., teaching persons how to perform a physical skill) can be best done *after* the various concepts of our discipline have been studied. In other words, physical education is the study of the many concepts and knowledges that relate to people and their movements. Although this study may be applied in teaching others how to move more efficiently, and efficient movement is one end result, it is not the only one.

DISCIPLINE OR PROFESSION – WHAT DIFFERENCE DOES IT MAKE?

If you are becoming discouraged by our lengthy discussion of the discipline and the profession of physical education, remember that these are vital matters for you and your future. One of the past problems in our field has arisen from the idea that physical education should be a science; some said that we should confine our energies to discovering new ways to perform a skill, new ways to strengthen muscles, new ways to discover new facts. Others have said that we should call our work an art, using what knowledge we have to teach others better ways to move and to perform skills. If physical education is defined as a discipline that studies the impact of many forms of movement upon both individuals and groups, it logically follows that the nature of physical education will involve various kinds of workers—scholars and researchers as well as teachers. Thus, some physical educators are primarily scientists (that is, scholars or researchers), while others are primarily professional educators (teachers or performers).

DEFINITION OF A PHYSICAL EDUCATOR

Earlier you were given our definition of physical educators: persons who possess breadth and depth of knowledge and skill concerning at least one key concept of vigorous human movement so that they can function as scholars, researchers, and/or professional educators. According to this definition, professional dancers or athletes are physical educators. Athletic coaches are physical educators. Teachers of activity skills are physical educators. Motor learning professors, who devote their time to laboratory research involving how animals (including humans) learn to perform, are also physical educators. At this time, however, the majority of physical educators are teachers, in that their major effort is devoted in instructing others about human movement.

THE BODY OF KNOWLEDGE IN PHYSICAL EDUCATION

In 1967, Fraleigh presented a model of the academic subject matter that should compose the discipline of physical education. Because this model seems to summarize what was said by the other authorities cited in this chapter, his ideas will be presented in some detail.

According to Fraleigh, physical education is a discipline that "attempts to investigate exercise, games, sports, athletics, aquatics, gymnastics, and dance in order to understand their uses and meanings to and for individuals and groups" (Fraleigh 1967, p. 34). The investigation of these various movement forms serves as the central core of our interest. Each of these movement forms relates to five key areas in the body of knowledge. These five areas are: (1) physiological development, (2) psychomotor development, (3) psychological development, (4) biomechanical development, and (5) sociological influences. In turn, each of of the areas can be more fully explained by listing the knowledges and understandings that compose them (which he calls the substantive content). Figure 5.2 shows these relationships.

It is now possible to combine the earlier discussion of the three domains that constitute the body of knowledge with Fraleigh's five areas in the discipline of physical education. Figure 5.3 depicts this relationship.

PREVIEW OF THE NEXT CHAPTERS

The substantive content of physical education will be examined in greater detail in the next five chapters. The concepts will be presented, along with the facts necessary to understand these concepts. A description of those courses that are designed to teach these concepts is given. Evaluative devices are presented in the instructor's guide. We hope that your instructor will find it possible to use them; comparing your results with those of other prospective physical education majors will enable you and your adviser to evaluate your present status more effectively.

YOUR AIM

What is your aim for this course—and for your career? It should be competence in the field for which you are best suited. Even if you already teach swimming, or have been a successful team captain or camp counselor, or were a student leader in physical education class in high school, you are not yet a physical educator. A person who can *do* things expertly is a technician. Nothing is wrong with being a technician—as a matter of fact, ours would be a better world if we had more of them. You are embarking on the training to be a scholar/researcher/professional educator in an academic discipline. The competent workers in physical education are persons who know about the human intellect as well as the body, about motor

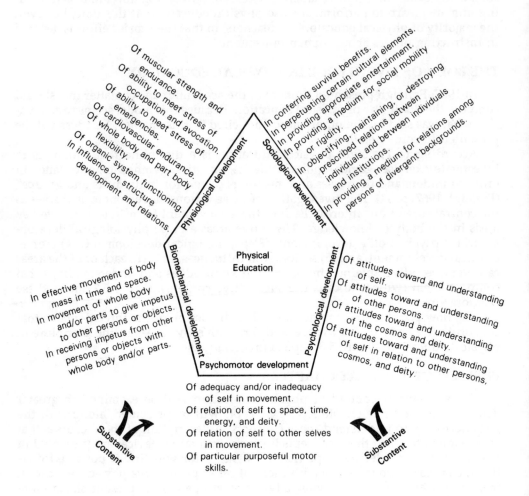

Physical
Education

Of muscular strength and
endurance.
Of ability to meet stress of
occupation and avocation.
Of ability to meet stress of
emergencies.
Of cardiovascular endurance.
Of whole body and part body
flexibility.
Of organic system functioning.
In influence on structure
development and relations.

Physiological development

Sociological development

In conferring survival benefits.
In perpetuating certain cultural elements.
In providing appropriate entertainment.
In providing a medium for social mobility
or rigidity.
In objectifying, maintaining, or destroying
prescribed relations between
individuals and between individuals
and institutions.
In providing a medium for relations among
persons of divergent backgrounds.

Biomechanical development

In effective movement of body
mass in time and space.
In movement of whole body
and/or parts to give impetus
to other persons or objects.
In receiving impetus from other
persons or objects with
whole body and/or parts.

Psychomotor development

Psychological development

Of attitudes toward and understanding
of self.
Of attitudes toward and understanding
of other persons.
Of attitudes toward and understanding
of the cosmos and deity.
Of attitudes toward and understanding
of self in relation to other persons,
cosmos, and deity.

Of adequacy and/or inadequacy
of self in movement.
Of relation of self to space, time,
energy, and deity.
Of relation of self to other selves
in movement.
Of particular purposeful motor
skills.

Substantive
Content

Substantive
Content

FIGURE 5.2. Concepts and substantive content related to the discipline of physical education. Adapted from W. P. Fraleigh, Toward a conceptual model of the academic subject matter of physical education as a discipline. *NCPEAM Proceedings* (1967): 36. Used by permission.

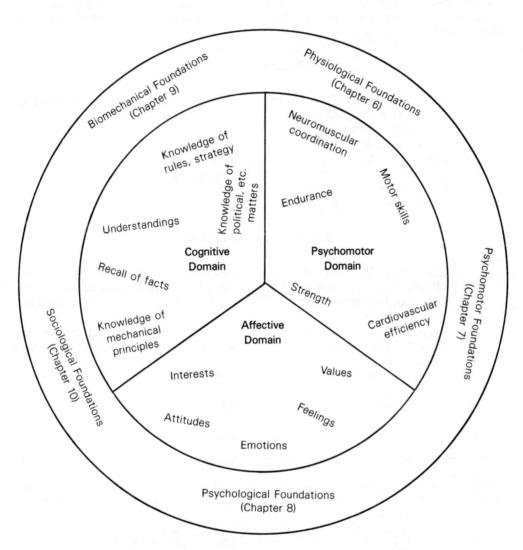

FIGURE 5.3. Body of knowledge in physical education.

skills, and about the psychology of motor activity. They understand the importance of physical movement in modern society (and can convince others of its value). To plan to be less than competent in the academic discipline of physical education is to plan to be less than the best. We hope you are striving to win, not merely to finish the race.

Student Activities

1. Survey a number of people in your college or hometown. Ask their opinions of these questions:
   a. What is physical education?
   b. What is athletics?
2. Read one article on one of these topics:
   a. Movement education (or human movement)
   b. Sport science (or sport education)
   c. Fitness—our primary aim.

Statements for Class Discussion

1. Since the public is sometimes confused about the values of physical education, we should not let them tell us what to do or how to do it.
2. Learning to move (to run, jump, etc.) is more important than learning how to play a game.
3. Regardless of the title given to physical education—subject, profession, academic discipline— you learn how to play and coach sports when you major in it.
4. The better an athlete you are, the more logical it is that you should major in physical education.
5. Better technicians make better teachers.

Bibliography

Abernathy, R., and Waltz, M. A. 1964. Toward a discipline: First steps first. *Quest* 2 (April): 1-7.

Benveniste, S. 1971. A case for physical education. *The Physical Educator* 28 (March): 43-45.

Digennaro, J. 1971. The purpose of physical education in the '70s. *The Physical Educator* 28 (October): 125-126.

Doherty, J. P. 1965. Let's stop playing games. *The Physical Educator* 22 (March): 23.

Edwards, D. 1971. Let's be—sports. *The Physical Educator* 28 (December): 181.

Falls, H., and McKinney, W. 1970. A philosophy of research preparation for the physical educator. *Quest* 14 (June): 44-49.

Fraleigh, W. 1967. Toward a conceptual model of the academic subject matter of physical education as a discipline. *NCPEAM Proceedings*: 31-39.

Green, E. R. 1972. Dance—an activity or a serious discipline? *JOPERD* 43 (January): 91.

Henry, F. 1964. Physical education—an academic discipline. *NCPEAM Proceedings*: 6-9. Also published in *JOPERD* 35 (September 1964): 32-33.

Huelster, L. 1965. The body of knowledge in physical education. *The Physical Educator* 22 (March): 6-8.

Jensen, J. 1970. Perspective unlimited: A new undergraduate physical education major. *JOPERD* 41 (September): 83.

Laughlin, N. 1972. Physical education—2000 A.D. *The Physical Educator* 29 (October): 115.

Metheny, E., *et al.* 1967. Physical education as an area of study and research. *Quest* 9 (December): 73-78.

Morford, R. 1972. Toward a profession, not a craft. *Quest* 18 (June): 88-93.

Nixon, J. 1967. The criteria of a discipline. *Quest* 9 (December): 42-48.

Polidoro, J. R. 1973. The affective domain: Forgotten objective in physical education. *The Physical Educator* 30 (October): 136.

Rarick, G. L. 1967. The domain of physical education as a discipline. *Quest* 9 (December): 49-52.

Rivenes, R., ed. 1978. *Foundations of physical education.* Boston: Houghton Mifflin Co. Chap. 1. The education of the physical educator.

Singer, R. 1978. Future directions in the movement arts and sciences. *The Academy Papers* 12 (December): 17-26.

Thomas, J. C. 1969. What are the characteristics of a true profession? *The Physical Educator* 26 (March): 9.

Ulrich, C., and Nixon, J. 1972. *Tones of theory.* Reston, Va.: AAHPERD.

Whited, C. 1971. Sport science. *JOPERD* 42 (May): 21-25.

chapter 6
Physiological Foundations of Physical Education

INTRODUCTION

In Chapter 5, we presented Fraleigh's model for the body of knowledge in physical education. One of the segments outlined in that model is *physiological development*. More specifically, Figure 5.2 indicates that physical educators should know a great deal about muscular and cardiovascular strength and endurance, flexibility, functioning of organic systems, the influence of structural development, and meeting various stresses that occur in life.

This chapter presents a definition of physiological development and briefly traces its history as it has waxed and waned in importance through the years. An attempt will be made to convince you of the importance of physiological development to individuals and to the discipline of physical education. Course work in physiological development is discussed. Finally, you will be made aware of the Youth Fitness Test and the new health-related fitness test, two measures of physiological condition.

CONCEPTS TO BE GAINED FROM THIS CHAPTER

When you have mastered the material in this chapter, you will be able to demonstrate comprehension of these concepts:

1. Physiological development was and is an essential segment of the body of knowledge in physical education.

2. Because physiological development is based in large part on the physical sciences, it is appropriate that the medical profession was and is closely related to physical education.
3. The President's Council on Physical Fitness and Sports is a unifying force in the effort to promote participation in fitness and sport activities for persons of all ages.
4. The term "physical fitness" is interpreted in many different ways.
5. Physical educators must have knowledge about the structure and function of various body parts.
6. Physical educators must have the attitude that personal fitness is a desirable attribute for themselves, now and throughout life.

DEFINITION OF PHYSIOLOGICAL DEVELOPMENT

By its usual definition, *physiological development* means the process of growth and expansion of a living organism. As used in physical education, the term means the process whereby the human body gains in any or all of such physical aspects as size, strength, coordination, and endurance. Such development occurs as a result of maturation, nutrition, and exercise. Even ineffective professional physical education teachers can expect increased physiological development in their students, as the laws of nature see to that!

HISTORICAL OUTLINE OF PHYSIOLOGICAL DEVELOPMENT

Introduction

We sometimes forget that ancient civilizations stressed physical activities in their scheme of education. Early "physical education" taught children to hunt, fish, and prepare food. In Grecian times, the sons of noblemen and upper-class citizens spent their early years learning to move gracefully and efficiently (e.g., run, jump, throw the javelin, swim). Only after some years of physical training did a person begin to "train" the mind.

During the Middle Ages, the Church deliberately tried to subject the physical body to the control of the soul. Asceticism meant that the body was deliberately punished through fasting, self-inflicted wounds, and lack of sleep so that the mind might control it. (Some say asceticism is still with us, in the form of overeating to the point of obesity, smoking or drinking to excess, and lack of exercise.) The result was that the mind and body, while obviously part of the same person, could be separated. The mind and soul became the master of the body, and thus mental training was supreme.

American Focus to 1956

Educators, especially those concerned with younger children, became convinced that physiological development could not be separated from mental development. Chapter 4 has indicated how physical education was introduced in

American schools. The importance of physiological development to physical education in the 1800s can be judged by the use of the term "physical culture." Measurement of various body segments (anthropometry) was a direct result of considering biological development as a key objective in physical education.

Various terms, such as "organic vigor" and "physical fitness" have been used to describe this objective of physical education. Draft statistics of the United States in World War I showed that about one-third of all men were rejected for physical reasons. Even though many of these draft rejections were for reasons not remedied by physical education, the public supported increased school requirements because they believed that physical development would be enhanced.

During the 1930s, emphasis shifted from physiological development toward the development of desirable personal-social traits gained through participation in physical activities. In other words, it was believed that education should be *through* the physical rather than *of* the physical. There was a greater stress on participation as the goal, rather than on physical development. To some extent, this development was caused by the Depression, which forced many people to have more leisure time than they were prepared to cope with. "Carryover activities" (e.g., recreational activities that could be used in later life) were stressed much more than physical development. Even during these years, however, such diverse persons as Charles Atlas (of the "97-pound weakling" advertisements), Frederick Rand Rogers (developer of the Physical Fitness Index), and C. H. McCloy (who popularized the idea of "education *of* the physical") stressed the physiological objective, each in his own way. (Is it a measure of the low status of physical education to guess that most readers of this text will have heard of Charles Atlas, but not of Rogers or McCloy?)

In 1941, the United States again called up many men for service in the Armed Forces, with approximately the same 30 percent rejection rate. As is typical during wartime, physical fitness became a prized goal, and there was a shift in emphasis in physical education programs. When the war was over, fitness faded (both literally and figuratively!) and did not become a national concern again until 1956, when the President's Council on Youth Fitness was activated.

THE PRESIDENT'S COUNCIL ON PHYSICAL FITNESS AND SPORTS

In June of 1955, President Eisenhower hosted a luncheon for 30 sports personalities, government officials, and medical researchers (no physical educators were invited) to discuss the dismal showing of American youth in the Kraus-Weber muscular strength and flexibility test. The test was called a physical fitness test, but the poor showing of American youth in comparison with European youth was in the flexibility item. After subsequent meetings, Eisenhower established the President's Council on Youth Fitness in July 1956. Its role was to alert the public to physical fitness concerns; the first director was a public relations expert. In 1961, President Kennedy issued a call for a "national renewal of vigor and vitality" and appointed Bud Wilkinson, former Oklahoma football coach, as the director. The program emphasis was shifted to sponsorship of clinics for professional physical educators, development of tests and standards, and research grants to various experts and universities. The Advertising Council began and continues a valuable public relations campaign on the fitness council's behalf. In 1963, Kennedy changed the council's name to the President's Council on Physical Fitness; this narrowed the focus of efforts to that of physical activity for persons of all ages and in all settings (school, community, and outdoor recreation).

The council was continued under President Johnson, although he was not as personally motivated as Kennedy had been. Different directors—Stan Musial, baseball superstar, and James Lovell, astronaut—were named in 1964 and 1967, respectively. In 1968, the name was again changed, this time to the present President's Council on Physical Fitness and Sports. This indicated a concern for sport participation as well as for physical fitness for all Americans.

Under Presidents Nixon, Ford, and Carter, the influence of the council continued to be felt. The professional staff, drawn primarily from AAHPERD members, was expanded. Annually, the council issued dozens of films, filmstrips, audio tapes, and publications and sponsored regional fitness clinics, industrial fitness conferences, and medical symposia. It maintained the recognition program (the awarding of certificates, emblems, and pins) for participants in 40 different sporting activities, from archery, biathlon, and cycling through wrestling and yachting. It attempted in every way to convince Americans of all ages that physical fitness and sport participation lead to desirable physiological development.

Results of the Fitness Emphasis

Vigorous exercise seems to have positive health benefits. A 1979 Public Health Service report credits the emphasis on physical exercise and fitness with slowing the trend toward a sedentary life style. In addition, there has been a 14 percent decrease in fatal heart disease among Americans in the last few years; some believe it can be traced to the improvement in exercise and diet and the reduced smoking patterns of adults, with exercise being mentioned as the most significant change.

In the years 1958-1965, substantial gains were made by Americans who took the AAHPERD Youth Fitness Test. In fact, the test standards were revised upward twice (1965 and 1975). Originally, European girls were slightly better than same-age American boys in six items of the AAHPERD test, but by 1965 this was no longer true.

Currently, over 18 million American young people aged 7-15 annually take the Youth Fitness Test, with over 700,000 of them earning emblems signifying superior performance. The period 1965-1980 has seen no substantial gain in scores for boys, however, and girls have shown improvement in only 7 of 40 scores (Reiff and Hunsicker, 1976). The youth fitness level, as measured by this test, has stayed the same.

The Youth Fitness Test has received some criticism, primarily because it measures performance-related fitness. In 1980, after many years of research and testing, AAHPERD published the Health-Related Physical Fitness Test. The difference between the two tests was summarized by Falls (1980, p. 25):

> Health-related means those aspects of physiological and psychological functioning which are believed to offer the individual some protection against degenerative type diseases, such as coronary heart disease, obesity, and various musculoskeletal disorders. . . . Performance fitness includes

those qualities of functions that provide the individual with the ability to participate in sport activities with greater power, strength, endurance, skill, etc. than otherwise. . . .

Whether the new test will become as popular as the old one remains to be seen.

Adult participation in exercise and sports has increased tremendously since 1956. Reasons for the boom have been many. The need of Presidents Eisenhower and Kennedy for a personal exercise program was certainly important, as was the increased emphasis by physicians on preventive medicine during this period. The extensive public relations campaign conducted by the President's Council (1973) showed the following facts:

1. Fifty-five percent of adult Americans regularly exercised, but a great percentage of these did not meet the minimum standards of frequency or effort recommended by the Council.
2. Walking was the most popular form of exercise, followed in order by bicycle riding, swimming, calisthenics, and jogging.
3. One-half of the people who exercised did so for health reasons.
4. In sport participation, bowling was the leading activity (20 percent of Americans participating). Others were swimming (18 percent), golf (9 percent), softball (8.5 percent), tennis (6 percent), and volleyball (5 percent).

A later study by the President's Council (1979) has confirmed the fact that there is a boom in adult participation. The number of adult runners has grown from a few in 1960 to 6 million in 1972 to 11 million in 1975 and 17 million in 1978. The number of racquetball players rose from 50,000 in 1970 to 3.1 million in 1978—a truly phenomenal increase. Swimming, tennis, golf, weightlifting, and other sports have all seen increased participation. It is estimated that one of every three Americans engages in over 200 minutes per week of vigorous physical activity.

Thus sport and exercise participation by Americans of all ages is truly at an all-time high. Even though there is still room for improvement, most experts believe that the percentage of participation will slowly continue to rise, and that as a nation we will never revert to the former pattern of confusing modern civilization with sedentary life style.

THE IMPORTANCE OF PHYSIOLOGICAL DEVELOPMENT

"People are physical beings"—this statement is trite because it is obvious. Since the dawn of recorded history, people have grown greatly in knowledge, while the physical body has undergone much less change.

Body evolution has been gradual, but our style of living has seen drastic change. Once the body was the mechanism by which people survived. They had to be cunning and strong enough to trap and kill animals for food; they had to know what, when, and how to plant; they had to learn to construct dwellings for shelter from the elements. The body was the key to accomplishment. Today, on the whole, it is the emerging and "less civilized" nations who use their physical prowess for survival. The rest of us devise new ways to do less physical work. An eminent cardiologist once said, "Golf is a stupid way to interrupt a walk." He clearly had not reckoned with electric golf carts, which permit us to play golf without even bothering to walk!

The idea that "what we don't use, we lose" is perhaps the chief reason why biological development remains a key objective in physical education. In primitive societies, biological development was taken care of by the process of survival. In our society, we must remain physically active to maintain strength, muscle tone, endurance, flexibility. Thus, the development of the physical body becomes even more important as our world becomes more automated and as we attain higher standards of living, because a higher standard of living usually means less physical work.

Physical activity and its benefits to humans have long been studied by specialists. Although some will have reservations, the large majority of physicians and exercise physiologists will agree with this summary by Wilmore (1980, p. 5):

> Regular exercise is necessary to develop and maintain an optimal level of good health, performance, and appearance. It can increase an individual's physical working capacity by increasing muscle strength and endurance; by enhancing the function of the lungs, heart and blood vessels; by increasing the flexibility of joints; and by improving the efficiency or skill of movement.

For many adults with sedentary occupations, physical activity provides an outlet for job-related tensions or mental fatigue. It also aids in weight control or reduction, improves posture, contributes to a youthful appearance, and increases general vitality. Active individuals appear to have fewer heart attacks than their less active counterparts. Furthermore, if an active individual does suffer an attack, it probably will be less severe, and chances of survival are greater.

Additionally, more than 50 percent of lower back pain or discomfort is due to poor muscle tone and lack of flexibility of the lower back and to inadequate abdominal muscle tone. In many instances, this disability can be prevented or corrected by proper exercise. And finally, much of the degeneration of bodily functions and structure associated with premature aging seems to be reduced by frequent participation in a program of proper exercise.

One of the problems that physical educators have had is convincing the public of the values of physical fitness. The literature is so vast and scattered that it is exceedingly difficult for an individual to keep informed. The President's Council on Physical Fitness and Sports has attempted to educate physical educators, who, in turn, will help inform the public concerning such findings as these:

1. A person's general learning potential for a given level of intelligence is increased or decreased in accordance with the degree of physical fitness. For example, in a California high school noted for its physical fitness program, boys in the top fitness groups obtained higher school grades by a 20:1 ratio, while the boys in the bottom 25 percent of fitness scores had a lower grade average than the average of all boys. High physical fitness is

not a guarantee of superior mental achievement, but the evidence is overwhelming that it relates to general learning potential (Clarke 1971, pp. 9-11).

2. Positive (favorable) relationships are shown between higher fitness levels and personality and social characteristics. For example, boys scoring high on physical-motor tests tend to be popular with peers, are extroverts and leaders, are more tolerant of others, etc. Boys low on physical-motor tests tend to feel inferior, insecure, and defensive, and possess other negative characteristics. Thus, in enhancing self-concepts and acceptance by peers, higher fitness levels are of value to boys (Clarke 1972, pp. 11-12).

Whether the material cited by Clarke is important is a somewhat controversial subject among physical educators. Though the facts are valid and reliable, we really have not ascertained the cause-effect relationship. Are superior mental achievement and positive personality and social characteristics a result of higher fitness levels, or do persons already possessing these attributes seek physical prowess, too? Do the same facts (regardless of their implications) hold true for females? These questions must be answered by scholars and researchers in physical education.

Another problem facing physical educators is dispelling the belief that all activities are equally good in developing fitness. Table 6.1 summarizes the thoughts of seven nationally known physical fitness experts (all physicians) as they rated 14 sports and exercises. It clearly shows that different activities have differing physiological values, using physical fitness and general well-being as the criteria. A rating of 21 points indicates maximum benefit. It was assumed that exercise was taken at least four times per week, 30-60 minutes per session.

The implications of this discussion of physical fitness are clear. Physical educators must be able to exert a positive influence on persons of all ages toward exercise. We must be able to document its benefits. Finally, we must be prepared to help persons learn psychomotor skills so that they can enjoy what they are doing.

EDUCATION OF THE PHYSICAL

Earlier in this chapter, the phrases "education *of* the physical" and "education *through* the physical" were used. The contrast between these phrases has stemmed from the term "physical education." To many professionals, "physical" implies that the primary goal of our discipline is education *of* the physical, that is, that persons should learn how to move so that their growth and development may be aided. The cognitive or affective benefits are of secondary importance. Advocates of education of the physical assert that physical fitness is our unique objective because no other discipline claims to improve the physiological aspect of the person; it is the only objective we can prove through accomplishment. Though physical educators may disagree that physiological development is the most important objective, they do agree that satisfactory development and maintenance of the muscles, heart, lungs, nervous system, and organic systems are essential for personal survival.

TABLE 6.1. RATINGS OF 14 SPORTS AS TO THEIR PHYSICAL FITNESS AND GENERAL WELL-BEING BENEFITS

	JOGGING	BICYCLING	SWIMMING	SKATING (ICE OR ROLLER)	HANDBALL/SQUASH	SKIING-NORDIC	SKIING-ALPINE	BASKETBALL	TENNIS	CALISTHENICS	WALKING	GOLF*	SOFTBALL	BOWLING
Physical fitness														
Cardiorespiratory endurance (stamina)	21	19	21	18	19	19	16	19	16	10	13	8	6	5
Muscular endurance	20	18	20	17	18	19	18	17	16	13	14	8	8	5
Muscular strength	17	16	14	15	15	15	15	15	14	16	11	9	7	5
Flexibility	9	9	15	13	16	14	14	13	14	19	7	8	9	7
Balance	17	18	12	20	17	16	21	16	16	15	8	8	7	6
General well-being														
Weight control	21	20	15	17	19	17	15	19	16	12	13	6	7	5
Muscle definition	14	15	14	14	11	12	14	13	13	18	11	6	5	5
Digestion	13	12	13	11	13	12	9	10	12	11	11	7	8	7
Sleep	16	15	16	15	12	15	12	12	11	12	14	6	7	6
Total	148	142	140	140	140	139	134	134	128	126	102	66*	64	51

Reprinted from *Medical Times*, May 1976.

*Ratings for golf are based on the fact that many Americans use a golf cart and/or caddy.

THE PENDULUM

The term "pendulum" is used to describe how interest in biological development as an objective of American physical education swings back and forth. The comments in Chapter 4 and in this chapter suggest that this alternating movement is common. The future looks much brighter for those who believe that the development of the body is our most important objective. The present public awareness of the values of exercise (as widely advertised on television and in the press) likely will continue. The medical profession seems to be more aware of the value of preventive medicine and the role of the physical educator in this regard. Interest is great in isometric and isotonic exercises, jogging, aerobics, and the President's Council on Physical Fitness and Sport. All of these factors will continue to promote physical development at all age levels. Presently, a popular concern is ecology; human ecology is seen to be as vital as environmental ecology.

LEARNING ABOUT PHYSIOLOGICAL DEVELOPMENT

The learning experiences related to this concept in physical education include both activity and theory courses. Probably no two colleges or universities require the same courses; even if the course titles are the same, the course content may differ. Therefore, the experiences listed below are examples of those courses most commonly included in professional preparation curricula.

Activity Courses

Conditioning. Many schools require physical education majors to take a class in which the goals are to improve the student's own physical condition and at the same time learn the techniques of helping others do the same. Exercises and routines designed to improve strength and endurance of the muscular system and the cardiorespiratory system are featured. You can test your attitude toward physical education by making an honest appraisal of your current conditioning efforts. Many of you are now in the best physical condition of your life; as you grow older, you will tend to become less physically active. If you look upon physical conditioning (not necessarily calisthenics, but any type of vigorous activity) as difficult, boring, and unnecessary, you may need to reconsider your future involvement in physical education.

Theory Courses

General Biology or Zoology. Most colleges and universities require an introductory course in this subject; the student is generally exposed to the organizational structure of the animal kingdom and the facts and concepts that underlie the discipline of biology.

Chemistry. As with general biology, an introductory course in chemistry is often required of physical education majors so that they can more fully understand the various chemical reactions that take place in the body.

Human Anatomy. This course consists of a thorough study of the various anatomical features—bones, joints, muscles, nerves—as found in the body. Much memorizing is involved in the study of anatomy. Some details may seem irrelevant now, but when you become a physical educator your attitude will change, because the human body will then be an essential focus of your concern. If at all possible, work in a laboratory with human cadavers should be a part of the anatomy course.

Human Physiology. The workings of the body— circulation, respiration, digestion, nervous control of movement, and growth—are the typical areas of concentration in this course.

Sometimes the anatomy and physiology courses are combined. This is logical in one respect, because the body itself cannot be divided and still function properly. The common problem, however, is that there is seldom enough time in one course for comprehensive study of the mass of details, facts, and concepts needed; thus students in such a combined course may not gain an in-depth understanding.

Physiology of Exercise. From the title, it should be obvious that this course is essential to members of our discipline. The functions of the body before, during, and after exercise must be studied by all physical educators. A typical text (Shaver 1981) contains chapters about these topics: skeletal muscles, energy and metabolism, respiration, heart, systemic circulation, neural control, temperature regulation, altitude, nutrition and weight control, ergogenic (work-producing) aids, sex differences, preadolescent and competitive sports, aging, and physical conditioning.

PHYSIOLOGICAL DEVELOPMENT AND YOU

As noted in Chapter 2, several schools give screening tests to major students in the area of biological development. The most common measurement is a physical fitness test. As you might expect, physical fitness is defined differently by different experts, and thus there are numerous tests. The AAHPERD Youth Fitness Test has been given to thousands of students of all ages. Chances are that you have already taken it.

We mentioned earlier the new health-related physical fitness test. Rather than measuring six performance skills as the present Youth Fitness Test does, this latter test assesses:

1. Cardiovascular function, as measured by a distance run of 1 mile or 1.5 mile, or a run lasting 9 or 12 minutes, depending upon age
2. Body composition, as measured by skinfold fat thickness in the tricep and subscapular areas of the body
3. Abdominal and low back-hamstring musculoskeletal function, as measured by modified and timed sit-ups, and by a sit and reach.

Each of these tests is important to you in two ways: (1) assessment of your own performance and health-related status and (2) familiarization with the test administration and interpretation. Complete directions for each test are given in the instructor's guide available with this text; we hope that your instructor will provide the opportunity for you to take the tests.

Student Activities

1. In your school library, try to find the physiological periodicals listed in Table 3.2 (p. 17). If you have time, read one article in each periodical.

2. Interview three or four physical educators. Ask their opinion on whether we should be more concerned with education *of* the physical or education *through* the physical. You may want to read the section, "Historical Background of Sport Psychology" in Chapter 8 before asking this question.
3. Observe and/or assist in physical fitness testing.
4. Note the extreme difference possible in growth and development by observing a group of children who are the same chronological age. Measure height, weight, length of arms, etc., if possible.

Statements for Class Discussion

1. Because some psychomotor elements (endurance, strength, etc.) tend to decline with age, while cognitive elements (knowledge, concepts, etc.) do not, the school should only be concerned with intellectual subjects.
2. Professional physical educators who are obese, out of shape, or who smoke should lose their jobs.
3. Departments should allow majors to remain in the program only if they exhibit:
   a. Satisfactory scores in physical fitness
   b. Normal or above normal physical growth and development
   c. No visible physical defects
   d. No grade lower than "C" in anatomy, physiology, or physiology of exercise.
4. Departments should make every major take and pass a physical fitness test just before he or she graduates.
5. Everybody is for physical fitness.
6. When I get the urge to exercise, I lie down until it passes.

Bibliography

AAHPERD. 1980. *Lifetime health related physical fitness: Test manual.* Reston, Va.: AAHPERD. 76 pp.

Brynteson, P. 1978. Fitness for life: Aerobics at Oral Roberts University. *JOPERD* 49 (January): 37-39.

Clarke, H. H., ed. 1971. The totality of man. *Physical Fitness Research Digest* 1, 3 (October); 1972. 2, 1 (January).

————, ed. 1979. Update: Physical activity and coronary heart disease. *Physical Fitness Research Digest* 9, 2 (April): 1-25.

DeGuzman, J. 1979. Dance as a contributor to cardiovascular fitness and alteration of body composition. *JOPERD* 50 (April): 88-91.

Ellfeldt, L. 1977. Aerobic dance (not really dance at all). *JOPERD* 48 (May): 45-46.

Falls, H. 1980. Modern concepts of physical fitness. *JOPERD* 51 (April): 25-27.

Gutin, B. 1980. A model of physical fitness and dynamic health. *JOPERD* 51 (May): 48-51.

Heck, K. 1980. Nutrition, diet, and weight control for athletes. *JOPERD* 51 (June): 43-45.

Hein, F., and Ryan, A. 1960. The contributions of physical activity to physical health. *Research Quarterly for Exercise and Sport* 31 (May): 263-285.

Kennedy, J. F. 1960. The soft American. *Sports Illustrated* 15 (December 26): 15-17.

Larson, L. A., and Michelman, H. 1973. *International guide to fitness and health.* New York: Crown.

Levitt, S. 1973. The limitations of training: Some implications for physical educators. *The Physical Educator* 30 (May): 89-90.

Lopez, R. 1980. Weight loss and diet in wrestling. *The Physical Educator* 37 (October): 131-139.

McDermott, B. 1975. Exercise you later, alligator. *Sports Illustrated* 42 (April 21): 36-42.

Pollock, M., and Blair, S. 1981. Exercise prescriptions. *JOPERD* 52 (January): 30-35.

President's Council on Physical Fitness and Sports. 1973. National adult physical fitness survey. *President's Council on Physical Fitness and Sports Newsletter* (May): 1-3.

————. 1979. Situation report on exercise in the United States. *President's Council on Physical Fitness and Sports Newsletter* (July): 3; (October): 4.

————. 1979. Nation's improved lifestyle linked to fitness boom. *President's Council on Physical Fitness and Sports Newsletter* (December): 3.

Rarick, G. L. 1968. Exercise and the growing years. In fact and fancy. P. B. Johnson, ed. *JOPERD* 39 (November-December): 37.

Reiff, G. 1980. Physical fitness guidelines for school age youth. *President's Council on Physical Fitness and Sports Newsletter* (March): 8.

Reiff, G. G., and Hunsicker, P. A. 1976. Youth fitness: 1975. *Update* (June): 5.

Shaver, L. G. 1981. *Essentials of exercise physiology.* Minneapolis, MN: Burgess Publishing Company. 310 pp.

Simpson, J. L. 1978. Dance and the athlete: An interview. *JOPERD* 49 (June): 20-21.

Tompkins, R. N. 1970. The swing of the pendulum—how wide? *The Physical Educator* 27 (October): 124.

Weiblow, J., et al. 1978. Nutrition and women in sports. *The Physical Educator* 35 (October): 124-126.

Wilmore, J. 1980. Exercise in the promotion of health in the adult population. *President's Council on Physical Fitness and Sports Newsletter* (March): 5.

chapter 7
Psychomotor Foundations of Physical Education

INTRODUCTION

The psychological foundations of physical education may be divided into two areas—psychomotor skills, and sport psychology. Sport psychology will be the subject of Chapter 8, while this chapter will focus on psychomotor skills.

Earlier, we quoted Fraleigh as saying that persons should know what psychomotor skills they themselves possess, how these skills can be successfully performed in different activities, and how these movements interact with the movements of others. This chapter will expand on these points through discussion of five concepts. Definitions will be given; the historical background, the importance of psychomotor skills, and the learning process will be presented. For your guidance, courses in this area that physical education majors need and how current skill ability can be assessed will be given.

CONCEPTS TO BE GAINED FROM THIS CHAPTER

When you have mastered the material in this chapter, you will be able to demonstrate comprehension of these concepts:

1. Although the curriculum and teaching methods have been altered, the importance of motor skills to our discipline has remained constant.
2. From an individual standpoint, skill in psychomotor movement is important for a healthful and emotionally satisfying life.
3. Psychomotor performance involves input, sensory receptors, central processing, muscular output, movement patterns, and feedback.

4. Psychomotor skills are learned in three phases.
5. Many factors cause differences in psychomotor performance among individuals and/or age groups. Researchers attempt to understand these factors and thus aid teachers and coaches.

DEFINITIONS RELATED TO PSYCHOMOTOR SKILLS

As in other areas, the psychomotor area can be discussed more intelligently when certain basic terms are understood. These are:

1. *Learning*—A relatively permanent modification of behavior as a result of training and environmental conditions that act upon an individual (Drowatzky 1981, p. 19).
2. *Psychomotor skills*—Those skills and abilities related to human movement that include both the mental and physical processes of the body. Some are basic movements (running, jumping), while others are combinations and refinements of these movements (high jumping, playing basketball).
3. *Activity class* (also called a gym class)—A class in which there is much physical activity, usually held in the gymnasium, in the pool, on the playing field, etc. The physical activity results in the learning of psychomotor skills.
4. *Movement education*—A method of teaching psychomotor skills in which students are allowed to discover their own ways to move.
5. *Command method*—The antithesis of movement education; using the command method, the teacher/coach gives precise directions on how to perform the activity or skill.
6. *Test battery*—A test consisting of a number of individual items (e.g., dribbling, free-throw shooting, pass for accuracy).
7. *Validity*—The extent to which a test measures what it is supposed to measure. A valid softball test, for example, will accurately measure how well you play softball.
8. *Reliability*—The extent to which a test consistently gives the same results under the same conditions. A reliable softball test gives virtually the same results if given on successive days to the same person.

HISTORICAL OUTLINE OF PSYCHOMOTOR LEARNING

Since the beginning of formal physical education as a school subject, the movement of the individual has been of supreme importance. Originally, students were taught calisthenics and formal drills in an effort to improve their health. These were done in a rather rigid pattern, with the teacher serving as a combination demonstrator and director. A logical assumption was that the teacher should know how to do the calisthenics and drills; this type of training was the type provided by early American physical education teacher-training schools.

As American physical education progressed, a strong feeling developed against this formal type of program. Games, leading to athletic contests, began to be popular, and the role of the teacher changed somewhat. Students were taught to perform the physical skills of a particular game and then spent part of the class period playing that game. The teacher's role became more that of a coach and observer.

In the 1930s, another dimension was added to physical education in the United States. Games and activities useful in later life (called "carryover" activities) were taught, in addition to the team games that were useful primarily in school. Thus, the physical education teacher was asked to become proficient in a variety of sport activities, so that he or she might teach them.

As movement education became popular in the 1950s, the role of the teacher in elementary school physical education was expanded. There was no set method of performing a skill; rather, the teacher became concerned with time, space, energy, and mass relationships.

The result of these changing emphases has given the physical education teacher great latitude in determining the content of the activity program. However, a good program will include activities from each of these categories:

1. Team games (e.g., volleyball, field hockey)
2. Individual and dual games (e.g., tennis, golf)
3. Rhythms (e.g., modern dance, social dance)
4. Self-testing or conditioning (e.g., weight training, jogging)
5. Aquatics (e.g., swimming, SCUBA)

Recently emphasis has been on altering the strategies for teaching psychomotor skills. Mosston, in his influential book *Teaching Physical Education* (1966), describes seven different teaching styles—command, task, reciprocal, small-group, individual-program, guided-discovery, and problem-solving. His premise is that, although most teaching is done by the command method ("do it this way"), this may not be the best teaching strategy in many instances. He points out that different goals require different teaching methods; a good physical education teacher will select the most appropriate method to fit the situation. Since Mosston, much research in teaching methods has been done. This has resulted in improved teaching, which in turn leads to improved performance.

THE IMPORTANCE OF PSYCHOMOTOR SKILLS

The values of efficient psychomotor movement are learned by children at an early age. A baby learns that movements like crawling, standing, walking, and talking enable it to meet certain goals, and they also produce a positive response from others. This effect continues throughout life, as we gain status by performing well on the athletic field, on the dance floor, or on the stage. Our physical and mental health is thus enhanced through psychomotor movements as we realize that we must move to survive, to work, and to play.

THE LEARNING PROCESS

Some persons believe that little or no mental effort is required for physical skill; the fact is that the mind and the body cannot be separated. For example, Bell (1970) points out that psychomotor movements include the central nervous system (brain and spinal cord), the peripheral nervous system throughout the body, and the muscles. Even simple reflex actions that are done without thinking (blinking) involve parts of the nervous system.

All physical educators are obviously interested in performance of psychomotor skills. Those who specialize in teaching, coaching, or research are vitally concerned with how persons learn skills. Robb (1970, pp. 50-56) has depicted the three phases in the manner shown in Table 7.1.

THE PERFORMANCE PROCESS

Exactly how do we perform a psychomotor skill? Rivenes (1978, p. 139) describes the process in this way:

1. *Cues* for action, either external (the sound of the starting gun) or internal (teeing a golf ball), which lead to
2. *Sensory reception* (awareness of body segments while in the starting position, or visual location of the golf ball), which lead to
3. *Central processing,* when the various inputs are organized into appropriate movement responses and lead to
4. *Muscular movements,* which in turn lead to
5. A *particular movement pattern* (the swing that results in hitting the golf ball). The final step in this performance is the
6. *Feedback* obtained at each step. Feedback enables the components of the performance to be modified and to become more successful.

TABLE 7.1. PHASES OF PSYCHOMOTOR SKILL ACQUISITION

PHASE	PURPOSE	COMMENTS
Cognitive	Learner must understand what is to be done.	Learner usually observes live demonstration or watches film. Learner can only think about few things at one time. Learner must concentrate on sequence of movements, not "correct form" shown in demonstration.
Fixation	Practice often to reduce conscious thought as to sequence, etc.	Usually requires more time than other two phases. Sometimes learner practices whole movement, sometimes works on the parts. Practice must be meaningful to produce results. Feedback is essential. Self-analysis is usually inaccurate, so a qualified teacher is most desirable. The length of practice periods varies with the task and the learner.
Automatic	Make psychomotor skills easier so that movements become almost unconscious.	Learner much less anxious or stressed over performance. Requires less "thinking," thus freeing learner to concentrate on strategy, etc. Difficult to change movement patterns once they reach automatic stage; qualified teacher most desirable.

Adapted from M. Robb, Man and sports—the acquisition of skill, *Quest* 14 (June 1970): 50-56.

Rivenes summarizes with the following model:

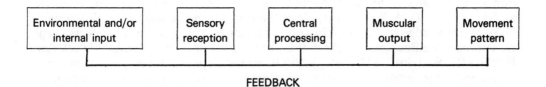

Researchers are vitally interested in factors that affect psychomotor performance. It is obvious that there are noticeable differences in psychomotor performance as infants progress through youth to adulthood. Four factors tend to be responsible for these changes—physical growth, biomechanical skills, physiological development, and the ability to process information (Thomas 1980).

Researchers are also interested in factors other than age. For example, do you know that some experiments have shown that when experienced basketball players practiced mentally (just thinking), they later shot more accurately than when they had previously practiced only physically? Do you know how motivation influences learning? Does knowing how to play badminton make it easier to learn tennis? Knowledge gained by studying these and other factors is used by teachers and coaches, with the final result being improved psychomotor performance.

LEARNING ABOUT PSYCHOMOTOR SKILLS

Courses that will help you understand more about your own and others' movement skills are discussed below.

Activity Courses

Team Games. The skills, rules, and strategy in these activities are usually covered: field hockey, touch football, soccer, speedball, basketball, volleyball, and softball.

Individual and Dual Sports. The skills, rules, and strategies in these activities are usually covered: archery, bowling, badminton, golf, track and field, tennis, and wrestling.

Rhythms. The skills and history of modern dance, folk dance, square dance, ballet, and social dance are usually covered.

Self-testing and Conditioning. The skills and basic principles of human movement, gymnastics (including tumbling and apparatus), track and field, weight training, "slimnastics," and physical fitness are usually covered.

Aquatics. The skills equivalent to those learned in an intermediate swimming course must usually be mastered, along with knowledge related to aquatics (principles of movement in water, small craft safety, and safety in swimming and diving).

Theory Courses

Psychomotor Learning. One of the most recent developments in the preparation of physical educators is the inclusion of a motor learning course on the undergraduate level. This is a result of the effort to make the physical education body of knowledge more directly applied to the teaching-learning process. Typical concepts studied include those found in the text *Motor Learning: Principles and Practices* (Drowatzky 1981): basic concepts, motor response development, nature of motor learning, feedback, timing, information processing, transfer, perception, personality and performance, motivation, and practice conditions.

Teaching Methods. For those planning to teach, at least one methods course (such as Teaching Techniques, or Methods and Materials) is required. These courses contain information about how to teach a category of activities (e.g., Methods and Materials of Tennis). Quite often such a course is taught by a specialist and includes detailed discussions of such topics as styles of teaching, creativity, movement education, maximum participation, describing and analyzing teaching, planning for teaching, evaluation, discipline and class control, legal liability, classroom management, and public relations (Dougherty and Bonanno 1979).

Related courses, discussed in other chapters, include anatomical and mechanical kinesiology and physiology of exercise.

PSYCHOMOTOR SKILLS AND YOU

According to most physical educators, the ability to perform the skills of an activity is highly desirable if one wishes to teach well. All physical educators will not be teachers, but the consensus is that those who can perform a minimum number of skills in a variety of activities will tend to be more successful in whatever phase of physical education they work.

A current popular belief in educational circles is that instruction is most beneficial when it is specifically geared to the needs of each student. Individualizing instruction requires the compiling of a great deal of information about each student. This is usually gained by some combination of testing (such as entrance exams, advanced placement exams, or aptitude tests), observation of the student's performance in an activity, and/or personal interviews. It is ironic that there are hundreds of research studies in physical education that concern the testing of physical skills, yet (as we showed in Chapter 2) only a few colleges or universities use any test (with the possible exception of a physical fitness test) to ascertain anything about the physical abilities of their beginning physical education majors. Even fewer schools give competency tests at the end of their students' training.

The problem is most acute when it concerns the beginning physical education major. Invariably, the majority of these students are well skilled in a few activities, yet unskilled in others. Wilson (1964, p. 65) points out:

> Frequently, all major students, upon entrance into an institution are placed in the same skills courses, regardless of previous experience. Once universal, today this pattern is questioned widely, since it frequently necessitates teaching geared near the beginning level. Such required instruction wastes the time of the highly skilled student.

As costs of education continue to escalate, what Wilson said many years ago is even more important today. Some departments permit students to take a battery of psychomotor tests; these give students the opportunity to "pass out" of activity courses in which they already have skill.

Some students and teachers believe that a psychomotor skills test is not a valid way to rate a person's playing ability. In theory, a valid and reliable skills test should give the same results as a subjective rating by expert judges, but this is a controversial issue.

The instructor's guide contains directions for sport skills tests in the following activities: archery, badminton, basketball, bowling, football, golf, soccer, softball, swimming, tennis, track and field, volleyball, and wrestling. We hope you will take many or all of these tests, thus aiding in the selection process described in Chapter 2.

Student Activities

1. In your school library, try to find the *psychomotor* periodicals in Table 3.2 (p. 17). If you have time, read one article in each periodical.
2. Observe a class in which mentally, emotionally, and/or physically handicapped persons are being taught a psychomotor skill. Compare the procedures with those used for normal students.
3. Interview senior physical education majors. What do they think about the skills tests used at your school?

Statements for Class Discussion

1. Playing the game is the best way to determine how good a person is in physical skills.
2. Since it is possible to learn how to play basketball from a fellow student, it is a waste of money to hire a physical education teacher to teach basketball.
3. Some coaches may be excellent teachers of psychomotor skills; the same persons may be ineffective as physical education teachers.

Bibliography

Bell, V. L. 1970. *Sensorimotor learning.* Pacific Palisades, Cal.: Goodyear Publ. Co.

Buckellew, W. 1971. The role of perceptual organization, feedback and communication in the development of physical skill. *The Physical Educator* 28 (October): 29.

Colvin, C. 1974. Movement education and soccer. *The Physical Educator* 31 (October): 148-150.

Dougherty, N. J., and Bonanno, D. 1979. *Contemporary approaches to the teaching of physical education.* Minneapolis: Burgess Publ. Co.

Drowatzky, J. 1981. *Motor learning: Principles and practices.* Minneapolis: Burgess Publ. Co., 2nd ed.

Lay, N. 1979. Practical application of selected motor learning research. *JOPERD* 50 (September): 78-79.

Lockhart, A., and Singer, R. 1971. What do we mean by the expert in motor learning? *JOPERD* 42 (February): 34-37.

Mohr, D. R. 1960. The contributions of physical activity to skill learning. *Research Quarterly for Exercise and Sport* 31 (May): 321-350.

Mosston, M. 1966. *Teaching physical education.* Columbus, Ohio: Charles E. Merrill Publ. Co.

Nicklaus, J. 1977. Have a whale of a time. *Sports Illustrated* 44 (October 19): 44-46.

Poll, T. 1979. Dance, self esteem, and motor acquisition. *JOPERD* 50 (January): 64-65.

Richardson, A. 1967. Mental practice: A review and discussion. Part 1. *Research Quarterly for Exercise and Sport* 38 (March): 95-107; Part 2. 38: 263-273.

Rivenes, R. 1978. The psychological perspective. Pp. 133-163 in Rivenes, ed. *Foundations of physical education.* Boston: Houghton Mifflin Co.

Robb, M. 1970. Man and sports—the acquisition of skill. *Quest* 14 (June): 50-56.

Singer, R. 1977. Different strokes for different folks—teaching skills to kids. Pp. 45-62 in Thomas, J., ed. *Youth sports guide.* Reston, Va.: AAHPERD.

Stafford, E. G. 1972. Professional activity courses, mainstay of the physical education curriculum. *The Physical Educator* 29 (March): 17.

Tharp, R. G., and Gallimore, R. 1976. What a coach can teach a teacher. *Psychology Today* 9 (January): 75.

Thomas, J. R. 1980. Acquisition of motor skills: Information processing differences between children and adults. *Research Quarterly for Exercise and Sport* 51 (March): 158.

Torpey, J. E. 1971. Motor-perceptual development and physical education. *The Physical Educator* 28 (March): 11.

Whiting, H. T. A. 1972. Overview of the skill learning process. *Research Quarterly for Exercise and Sport* 43 (October): 266.

Williams, I. 1971. Effects of practice and prior learning on motor memory. *Journal of Motor Behavior* 3 (September): 205-211.

Wilson, R. M. 1964. Competency testing. *JOPERD* 35 (February): 64-66.

chapter 8

Psychological Foundations of Physical Education

INTRODUCTION

As mentioned earlier, psychological interest in sport and physical activity can be divided into two areas—psychomotor skills and sport psychology. Chapter 7 dealt with the former; this chapter will discuss the latter.

Fraleigh (see Chapter 5) has indicated that personal expression (which we prefer to call sport psychology) is a foundation area of physical education. He implies that physical educators should be concerned about their attitudes and understanding of themselves and others. Sport psychologists agree, and have devoted much time and effort in recent years to detailed study of athletes and nonathletes in numerous sport and physical activity situations. (It must be stressed that the psychological environment cannot be separated from the biological, biomechanical, and social environment; thus the material in Chapters 6-10 must be considered as an entity.)

This Chapter presents concepts, definitions, and historical background related to sport psychology. The importance of the topic, with the particular aspects studied by researchers and used by teachers/coaches, is emphasized. To close this chapter, specific courses basic to sport psychology are mentioned, along with a superficial means of assessing your interest in this area.

CONCEPTS TO BE GAINED FROM THIS CHAPTER

When you have mastered the material in this chapter, you will be able to demonstrate comprehension of these concepts:

1. Interest in sport psychology has stemmed from the belief that education through the physical is a legitimate objective of physical education.
2. Whether participation in athletics causes beneficial effects in competitors is an unresolved issue.
3. Regardless of the evidence, most physical educators and coaches are convinced that athletic participation is beneficial to participants.
4. Because of the interrelatedness of physical, intellectual, emotional, and social behaviors, sport psychologists have difficulty in making objective conclusions about the importance of a particular variable.

DEFINITIONS RELATED TO SPORT PSYCHOLOGY

Certain words and terms must be understood before we proceed with our discussion of sport psychology.

1. *Sport psychology*—The study of human behavior in sport and physical activity situations. It is not confined to athletic situations, but encompasses athletes and nonathletes who engage in sport and physical activity.
2. *Personal expression*—The outward appearance of the inner person.
3. *Psychosocial development*—An objective of physical education and athletic programs, wherein a person's behavior is positively influenced through participation in sport and physical activity.
4. *Character traits*—Characteristics of persons. In sport psychology, such traits as sportsmanship, character, aggression, emotional control, perception, and social status are studied.

HISTORICAL BACKGROUND OF SPORT PSYCHOLOGY

As indicated in Chapter 4, American physical education became a school subject in the 1850s, when it was seen as a means of improving the physical health of students. It was regarded in this way up through the era of anthropometric measurement of the 1880s. The influence of the "new" physical education in the early 1900s caused a shift in emphasis to programs featuring athletic games. The justification for this change was that American youth were much more interested in a games-type approach and that these games could be educational in nature. The vigorous competitive play found in physical education (especially athletics) was thought to be highly effective in teaching various desirable character traits. The term "education *through* the physical" (as opposed to "education *of* the physical," mentioned in Chapter 6) was used to describe this psychosocial objective.

Physical educators and coaches were quick to proclaim the educational value of physical education and especially athletics, but research supporting many of the claims was (and still is) lacking. Although interest in sport psychology began in Europe in the early 1900s, it was not until 1926 that C. R. Griffith's *Psychology of Coaching* was published in the United States, followed in 1928 by his *Psychology of Athletics* and in 1930 by Clarence Ragsdale's *Psychology of Motor Learning*.

Unfortunately, these publications created little interest in this subject. American coaches and physical educators were given little help from researchers until 1966, when the North American Society for Psychology of Sport and Physical

Activity was formed. From this date, the beliefs (that sports build character, that teamwork in athletics will carry over into later life, and others) related to the values of sport and physical activity have been subject to close scrutiny by many. For example, the relationship between personality traits and physical activity (particularly athletic competition) has been extensively studied, first by psychologists Ogilvie and Tutko of San Jose State University. They studied thousands of athletes of both sexes, all ages, and all skill levels, and served as consultants to athletes, coaches, and entire teams. Their Athletic Motivational Inventory, based on personality traits, has been used by coaches to select team members and to later motivate them to better performance.

Whether the personality trait approach is valid and reliable may be controversial. However, Ogilvie and Tutko have paved the way for the widespread use of sport psychologists as consultants to professional, college, and Olympic teams. Although this has been a common practice in Europe for many years, it is only since the mid-1970s that American sport psychologists have consulted with team members and have traveled with teams to major competitions. A growing number of sport psychologists are in private practice, consulting, writing, speaking, and conducting clinics for teams; one such person is a former All-American swimmer, who devotes his time to working with age-group, high school, and college swim teams.

THE VALUE OF SPORT AND PHYSICAL ACTIVITY TO PSYCHOSOCIAL DEVELOPMENT

Can physical education (which includes the competitive phase that we call athletics) alter personality, character, sociability, expression? For many years we have claimed that students gain these personal-social values from our program, but the evidence has never been conclusive. For example, Scott (1960) concluded that proof was lacking that physical activity caused beneficial psychological effects in persons, and Cowell (1960, p. 287) made the same observation in regard to the social dividends of physical activity. A closer look at each of these assertions should be enlightening to you.

Only in the past ten years have physical educators begun systematic research into the entire area of personal expression, using psychology, physiology, and sociology as the foundation sciences. Although it is much too early to assert that physical activity definitely does or does not cause personality and social changes, we do know much more now about the many parts that make up these broad areas. For example, as we showed in Chapter 7, physical activity is essential in learning motor skills, artd psychological development plays an important part in that learning. In turn, we know that motor skills are used as the basis of play activity for persons of all ages, and psychiatrists and physical educators agree that serious play (as opposed to aimless play) favorably influences the personality of persons (Menninger 1948, p. 343). It is wise to remember, however, that although play and sports have the potential for contributing positively to the attainment of emotional health, there are indications that, for some groups and for some individuals, under some circumstances, this might not be true. Layman (1972, p. 181) writes:

Sports are conducive to emotional health if they promote physical fitness. [But not all sports do.] They encourage healthy emotional development if the participant has enough skill to merit the approval and admiration of peers, and enough so that he can have a feeling of success. [But not all participants have enough skill.] They encourage healthy emotional development if the participant can use them for spontaneous expression of positive feelings and discharge of aggressive tensions. [But not all participants can do this.]

What have we learned about the effect of physical activity on psychological development? Usually we study groups of athletes, either by themselves or in comparison with groups of nonathletes. A sample of various findings by researchers shows the wide variety of conclusions that have been arrived at:

1. Male and female athletes are basically emotionally healthy, self-confident, able to cope with stress, leaders, tough-minded. Numerous other "desirable" personality traits are also attributed to them. But as they continue to compete, they also become less interested in personal concerns of others and more dominant (Ogilvie 1967, p. 48).
2. Male athletes tend to be extraverted and to possess greater general emotional control than do unathletic males. Women athletes are also extraverted, but show a lower level of emotional control than do men athletes (Kane 1972, p. 118).
3. Kistler (1957) showed that adult and college males who had varsity experience had a poorer attitude about sportsmanship than did those who had no varsity experience.
4. Lakie surveyed 228 athletes at three different colleges and concluded that "outcomes in sportsmanlike behavior may vary under different leadership and environment" (Lakie 1964, p. 497).
5. Thomas, Young, and Ismail (1973) felt that high school football players of high ability may undergo subtle personality modification during a season, but that the low-ability players are unaffected.
6. Collis (1972) developed a written aggression test and found that as male swimmers, gymnasts, and hockey and soccer players got older (entered high school) they became more aggressive. They had more disregard for sporting laws. The soccer and ice hockey players, especially, favored extralegal aggression.
7. Peterson, Weber, and Trousdale (1967) found that there were personality trait differences between women team sport participants when compared to women who competed in individual sports. Individual-sport women rated higher on dominance, adventurousness, sensitivity, introversion, radicalism, and self-sufficiency, and were lower on the sophistication trait.
8. O'Connor and Webb (1976) compared female college athletes (swimmers, gymnasts, basketball players, and tennis players) with a nonathletic group of college females, using the Cattell 16 PF test. They reported some

disagreement with earlier studies in that various groups scored significantly higher on such traits as intelligence, radicalism, group dependence, and self-control than other investigators' findings showed.

9. Snyder and Kivlin (1975) compared college women athletes with college women nonathletes to ascertain if the "girl jock" image was of concern to the athletes. They found that, on measures of psychological well-being and body image, the athletes were more positive; that is, they felt that sport participation was psychologically satisfying and rewarding. Female basketball players were as pleased with their body image as female gymnasts.

What can we say about the overall benefits of athletic competition? Most physical educators will agree with Alley (1974, p. 102):

> High school (male) athletics, if directed by coaches of resolute integrity dedicated to optimum development of their players as individuals, can be an exceedingly potent tool for developing desirable behavior patterns. . . .

We are certain that you have been convinced that competition "does something good" for participants. Study Table 8.1. It summarizes the assumed values of athletics and provides comments by critics. We make no attempt to prove anything; rather, we are indicating that it is difficult to show a cause-effect relationship.

TABLE 8.1. VALUE OF INTERSCHOLASTIC-INTERCOLLEGIATE ATHLETICS—AN ENIGMA

	ASSUMED VALUES	INCONSISTENCIES
Control	Participation helps develop self-control, self-discipline, etc.	Training rules, dress codes, conformity are dehumanizing. Teamwork doesn't breed individuality.
	Coaches, schools, and community, who know best, exert much control over athletes.	Who knows what is best? Title IX passed to force desirable changes.
	Athletics builds character.	Better to say, athletics reveals character. No proof it builds it.
	Society benefits from athletics. Entertainment occupies students' leisure time, athletes must stay in school to compete.	Is entertainment or education the reason for school athletics? No evidence that delinquency is reduced due to sport participation.
	Studies show athletes are superior to nonathletes in desirable personality traits.	No evidence that athletics causes desirable personal characteristics. "Ruthless selection" perhaps weeds out those lacking in such traits.
Competition	Life is competitive, and athletics is preparation for life.	"Win at all costs" is certainly not preparation for life in a democracy.
	Healthy (e.g., fair and vigorous) competition is valuable to all.	
	Those with success in competition are associated with desirable personality traits.	Studies show coaches want to win more than athletes; who is benefiting? "Ruthless weeding out" of unfit?

TABLE 8.1. (Continued)

	ASSUMED VALUES	INCONSISTENCIES
Social security	Athletes show increased social status.	
	Success in athletics increases chances to escape the ghetto.	Edwards, black sociologist, says no.
	One may increase one's social standing.	
	Good athletic program is of economic value to community or school.	Cost of scholarships, etc., means most college programs are not self-supporting.
		Relatively few students in any college get athletic scholarship aid.
Physical well-being	Athletes are in better physical condition than nonathletes.	Great variation among sports, and among individuals in same sport. Study shows intramural athletes are as well conditioned.
	Injury rate may be increased, but not appreciably.	In Germany, 10% of all hospitalized accidents due to sports, don't know U.S. figures.
Spirit value	Athletics promotes teamwork, cooperation, school spirit.	Can't show that participation in athletics voluntarily promotes teamwork cooperation.
	Students and alums are vitally interested in athletic prowess of school teams.	In some U.S. cities, fans so riotous that they are barred from watching.
Summary	Arguments used in supporting or attacking athletics are same ones used 50 years ago.	
	Physical education teachers and coaches have different philosophies and goals concerning athletics. When the same person has both roles, internal conflict often results.	
	Research in area is sparse and inconclusive.	
	Not able to support one side or the other with valid research.	

Adapted from C. R. Knicker, The values of athletics in schools: A continuing debate, *Phi Delta Kappan* 56 (October 1974): 116-120. Used by permission.

THE IMPORTANCE OF SPORT PSYCHOLOGY

Krotee has pointed out that there are many variables that influence psychomotor performance. He says (1980, p. 48) that sport psychologists must be:

1. Familiar with and able to effectively communicate performance expectations and knowledge or results to the primary and secondary participant
2. Responsible for designing and implementing a "training and practice package" to satisfy needs, goals, and performance objectives
3. Able to manipulate the learning environment progressively and systematically, including the integration of skill, strategy, and values of activity.

Figure 8.1 portrays the numerous variables studied by sport psychologists.

Taken together, Table 8.1 (Values of Athletics) and Figure 8.1 (Variables Related to Sport Psychology) clearly indicate the importance of sport psychology. Research concerning the parts (e.g., personality traits, aggression, motivation, etc.) has convinced physical educators, coaches, and psychologists that sport and physical activity does exert positive influences in the psychomotor and psychosocial areas. As Ismail (1972) asserts, the physical, intellectual, emotional, and social types of development are not independent, but are so closely related that the whole is more than the sum of its parts. Sport psychologists will continue to study the activity situation and the psychological attributes that affect performers. This research is important, because it will permit better performance and will

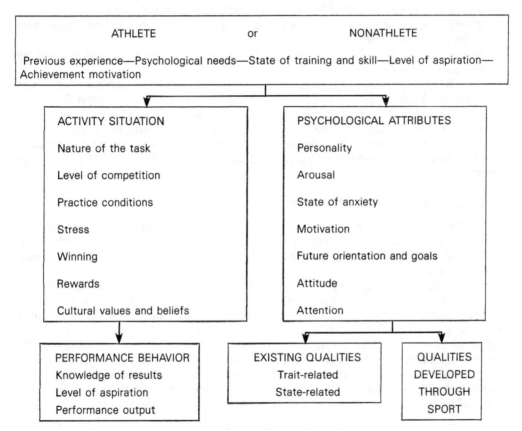

FIGURE 8.1. VARIABLES OF INTEREST TO SPORT PSYCHOLOGISTS. Adapted from M. L. Krotee and F. Hatfield, *The theory and practice of physical activity* (Dubuque, Iowa: Kendall-Hunt Publ. Co., 1979).

enable teachers/coaches to better help their students and athletes. Until we know more about the whole, we cannot justify the sweeping accolades made for the value of participating in sport and physical activity.

LEARNING ABOUT SPORT PSYCHOLOGY

Courses that a physical educator needs to enhance the understanding of sport psychology are listed below.

Introduction to Psychology. Study of individual and group characteristics and reactions. This will give a basic understanding of the psychological makeup of persons.

Introduction to Sociology. All schools offer this beginning course, which calls attention to the social and cultural forces that influence behavior.

Psychomotor Learning. This course, usually taught by physical educators, was described in Chapter 7.

Sport and Society. This course, usually taught by physical educators, will be described in Chapter 10.

Psychology of Coaching. This course applies to both the coaching of athletics and the teaching of physical education skills to nonathletes. A typical course, based on a contemporary text (Llewellyn and Blucker 1982) includes these topics: growth and development, personality and performance, techniques of motivation, anxiety and performance, information processing, aggression, mental preparation, practice factors, the coach as a counselor, coaching youth, high school and college athletes.

SPORT PSYCHOLOGY AND YOU

At this writing, there are no formal methods of assessing a person's current knowledge or standing in sport psychology variables. Many paper-and-pencil tests on personality traits have been given to physical education majors, athletes, teachers, and coaches.

Some informal subjective methods may be applied to assess your own competence in this area. Examine some of your attitudes: Is it necessary to make a contest of every game? Are you upset when you lose a friendly game? Is it worth it to play hard or do you prefer to just "play around"? Can you cite specific instances of athletics having positively influenced your life? Does the end (winning) justify the means (cheating)? Must you have officials when you play, or can you call your own fouls? Do you subscribe to the "winners never quit—quitters never win" philosophy? These questions have no absolute answers, but they represent the type of inquiry that is thought provoking for all sport participants.

Student Activities

1. In your school library, try to find the *psychological* periodicals listed in Table 3.2 (p. 17). If you have time, read one article from each periodical.
2. Survey one or more of the groups listed below. Ascertain what benefits, if any, they received from athletic competition. (Remember that their background will strongly influence their answers.) Report your results.
   a. Current athletes in your school (both male and female)

    b.   Students who have never gone out for athletics in college, but did so in high school

    c.   Students who have never turned out for athletics

    d.   Adults who have not competed in athletics for at least 15 years

3.   Ask nonmajors to describe the typical physical education major.

Statements for Class Discussion

1.   The best way to survive the competition of real life is to participate in athletics.

2.   Education *through* the physical is more important—and more valuable— than education *of* the physical.

3.   Education of the mind is more important than education of the body.

Bibliography

Alley, L. E. 1974. Athletics in education: The double-edged sword. *Phi Delta Kappan* 56 (October): 102-105.

Benagh, J. 1978. Rowdy spectators—the bad apples of sports. *Family Weekly* (June 4): 7-9.

Berkowitz, L. 1973. Sports, competition and aggression. *The Physical Educator* 30 (May): 59-61.

Brown, G. 1973. Winning one for the Ripper. *Sports Illustrated* 39 (November 26): 46.

Bruns, B. 1973. Psychologist in the lineup. *Human Behavior* 2 (June): 8-15.

Bunker, L., and Rotella, R. 1977. Getting them up, not uptight. Pp. 75-87 in Thomas, J., ed. *Youth Sports Guide*. Reston, Va.: AAHPERD.

Caldwell, S. F. 1972. Toward a humanistic physical education. *JOPERD* 43 (May): 31-32.

Check, J. F. 1970. The psychology of competition as it relates to the physical educator and the athletic coach. *The Physical Educator* 27 (October): 110.

Collis, M. L. 1972. Collis scale of athletic aggression. P. 68 in AAHPERD. *Abstracts of Research Papers*. Reston, Va.: AAHPERD.

Cowell, C. C. 1960. The contributions of physical activity to social development. *Research Quarterly for Exercise and Sport* 31 (May): 286-306.

Harris, D. V. 1975. Research studies on the female athlete: Psychological considerations. *JOPERD* 46 (January): 32-36.

Hellison, D. 1970. Physical education and the self-attitude. *Quest* 13 (January): 41-44.

Hoehn, R. 1971. The coach as a psychologist. *Scholastic Coach* 40 (April): 78.

Ismail, A. H. 1972. Integrated development. Pp. 1-37 in Kane, J. E., ed. *Psychological aspects of physical education and sport*. Boston: Routledge and Kegan Paul.

Kane, J. E. 1972. Personality, body concept and performance. Pp. 91-127 in Kane, J. E., ed. *Psychological aspects of physical education and sport*. Boston: Routledge and Kegan Paul.

Kenyon, G. 1968. Sociological considerations. *JOPERD* 39 (November-December): 31-33.

Kistler, J. 1957. Attitudes expressed about behavior demonstrated in certain specific situations occurring in sports. *NCPEAM Proceedings*: 55-59.

Knicker, C. R. 1974. The values of athletics in schools: A continuing debate. *Phi Delta Kappan* 56 (October): 116-120.

Kroll, W., and Lewis, G. 1970. America's first sport psychologist. *Quest* 13 (January): 1-4.

Krotee, M. L. 1980. Sport psychology. *JOPERD* 51 (November-December): 48-49.

———, and Hatfield, F. 1979. *The theory and practice of physical activity*. Dubuque, Iowa: Kendall-Hunt Publ. Co.

Lakie, W. 1964. Expressed attitude of various groups of athletes toward athletic competition. *Research Quarterly for Exercise and Sport* 35 (December): 497-503.

Layman, E. C. 1972. The contribution of play and sports to emotional health. Pp. 163-186 in Kane, J. E., ed. *Psychological aspects of physical education and sports.* Boston: Routledge and Kegan Paul.

Llewellyn, J. H., and Blucker, J. A. 1982. *Psychology of coaching: Theory and application.* Minneapolis: Burgess Publ. Co.

Menninger, W. C. 1948. Recreation and mental health. *Recreation* 42 (November): 340-346.

O'Connor, K. A., and Webb, J. L. 1976. Investigations of personality traits of college female athletes and nonathletes. *Research Quarterly for Exercise and Sport* 47 (May): 203-210.

Ogilvie, B. 1967. What is an athlete? *JOPERD* 38 (June): 48.

—— and Tutko, T. 1971. Sport: If you want to build character, try something else. *Psychology Today* 5 (October): 61-63.

—— and ——. 1972. Motivation and psychometric approach in coaching. Pp. 209-231 in Kane, J. E., ed. *Psychological aspects of physical education and sport.* Boston: Routledge and Kegan Paul.

Peterson, S. L., Weber, J. C., and Trousdale, W. W. 1967. Personality traits of women in team sports vs. women in individual sports. *Research Quarterly for Exercise and Sport* 38 (December): 686-690.

Ruffer, W. A. 1975. Personality traits of athletes: Part I (Bibliography). *The Physical Educator* 32 (May): 105. See also: (October): 161; (December): 213.

Scott, J. 1973. Sport and the radical element. *Quest* 19 (January): 71-77.

Scott, M. G. 1960. The contributions of physical activity to psychological development. *Research Quarterly for Exercise and Sport* 31 (May): 307-321.

Snyder, E., and Kivlin, J. E. 1975. Women athletes and aspects of psychological well-being and body image. *Research Quarterly for Exercise and Sport* 46 (May): 191-199.

Stevenson, L. 1975. Socialization effects of participation in sport. *Research Quarterly for Exercise and Sport* 46 (October): 287-301.

Thomas, T. D., Young, R. J., and Ismail, A. H. 1973. The effects of a football season on the personality of high school athletes. P. 67 in AAHPERD. *Abstracts of Research Papers.* Reston, Va.: AAHPERD.

chapter 9

Biomechanical Foundations of Physical Education

INTRODUCTION

> Biomechanics . . . involves both the study of the biological foundations for motion and the mechanical and physical laws which govern that motion. (Carr 1978, p. 129)

More specifically, Fraleigh has indicated that the physical educator should know about the effective and efficient (1) movement of body mass in relation to time and space (as in running, swimming, jumping), (2) movement of the whole body and/or parts to give impetus to other persons or objects (as in throwing, hitting), and (3) receipt of impulses from other persons or objects with the whole body and/or parts (as in catching, absorbing a blow from another person).

In an attempt to make this area meaningful, this chapter will present concepts, definitions, and the historical background leading to today's research and educational emphasis in applied mechanics. The importance of biomechanics, to both performers and teachers/coaches, will be discussed. Finally, courses that physical educators customarily take for knowledge in this area are given, followed by suggestions to assess your present knowledge in biomechanics.

CONCEPTS TO BE GAINED FROM THIS CHAPTER

When you have mastered the material in this chapter, you will be able to demonstrate comprehension of these concepts:

1. Teaching methods, directed either by the teacher/coach or of the movement-exploration type, result in movements that agree with the principles of biomechanics.
2. Biomechanics is an essential segment of the physical education body of knowledge because all psychomotor movements must conform to certain anatomical, physiological, physical, and mathematical facts and laws.
3. Researchers are able to advise performers and to better educate teachers and coaches through the use of sophisticated aids.

DEFINITIONS

Definitions of terms in the biomechanics area follow.

1. *Biomechanics*—According to Carr (1978, p. 96), this is the ". . . study of individuals and implements and their interactions with the environment. . . . In its fullest definition [it is the] science that studies and analyzes the effects on performance that those forces produce."
2. *Laws of motion*—The Newtonian laws (inertia, acceleration, action-reaction), which are the basis for examining and explaining how we move.
3. *Mechanics of action* (also called technique, or form)—". . . The general application of mechanical laws in an efficient manner" (Carr 1978, p. 124).
4. *Style*—"An individual's highly personal application of technique" (Carr 1978, p. 124).
5. *Anatomical kinesiology*—The study of gross anatomy, with the goal of understanding the movement of specific body parts during activity.
6. *Mechanical kinesiology*—The study of how and why body movement conforms to mechanical laws.
7. *Form*—An older term that implies conformity to a style of performance. In the past, form has been based on the performance style of champions, which may or may not be mechanically correct.

HISTORICAL BACKGROUND OF BIOMECHANICS

As mentioned in Chapter 4, early American physical education was marked first by athletic games played after school (coached by a playing captain) and later by formal exercises conducted in a rather strict routine. In both instances, students were told how to perform—that is, what the "proper form" was. Correct form depended on the way the champions did the skill or on principles derived from the study of human anatomy. Since the arms, legs, and trunk of the body are moved by muscles, the body was (and still is) considered a system of levers and forces. In this way movement could be scientifically related to mechanical principles.

Relationship of movement to scientific principles meant that physical educators had to know more than just human anatomy. The kinesiology texts of the 1900-1940 era, however, were primarily thorough reviews of anatomical kinesiology that gave little attention to such scientific principles as momentum and gravity. Since the 1940s, the emphasis has shifted. *The Scientific Principles of Coaching* (written by John Bunn, an engineer turned basketball coach), *Efficiency of Human Movement* by Marion Broer, and *The Mechanics of Athletics* by Geoffrey Dyson are three significant texts that caused physical educators to integrate physics, mathematics, and anatomy into what is called "mechanical kinesiology."

As mentioned in Chapter 7, movement education has been advocated by some physical educators since the 1950s. It is common knowledge that certain psychomotor skills (hitting a baseball or softball) are performed differently by different persons. In these skills, results are more important than "proper form." Students are encouraged to experiment. For example, if a person wanted to move from one place to another, he or she might walk, crawl, roll on the ground, hop, or walk backward. A ball does not necessarily have to be thrown with "correct" form, if another way is more effective. Movement exploration follows anthropomechanical principles; it seeks workable alternatives to a problem within the limits imposed by these principles.

Movement education has gained advocates, especially for lower elementary school programs. There are too many instances of persons succeeding without "proper form" for us to spend hours trying to copy an expert. There are so many individual differences (e.g., height, weight, strength, visual acuity, reaction times) that no one way is effective for everyone. Finally, too little is known to tell us the "best method" for any movement.

On the other hand, the great majority of champions conform to basic physical, anatomical, physiological, and mathematical principles in their important movements. Our problem has been that we have not understood the basics well enough and have had to learn from the experts. (A leading American high jumper was amazed when told that the Russians had published a several-hundred-page scientific book on that activity. "I didn't know there was that much to write about high jumping," he was reported to have said.)

The most recent development in biomechanics revolves around the use of sophisticated scientific equipment, enabling researchers, coaches, and teachers to evaluate psychomotor skill performance more accurately. The computer, high-speed cameras, force platforms, digitizers, strobe lights, and telemetric devices are some examples of these aids. Foreign countries, especially those in which athletic prowess is used to gain international prestige, have been well ahead of the United States in this regard; however, the 1980s will see biomechanical experts (as well as sport psychologists and exercise physiologists) become permanent members of American university and Olympic athletic development programs.

THE IMPORTANCE OF BIOMECHANICS

History tells us that athletic records are continually being broken. However, as Alley (1966, p. 68) reported:

> Most of the improvements in athletic performances that have resulted from radical changes in style have come about through trial and error or intuitive tinkering by persons with little sophistication in mechanics. These improvements are later explained *post facto* by persons with a knowledge in mechanics.

An outstanding example is the influence of Perry O'Brien in the shot put. Originally, shot-putters faced the direction of the put. O'Brien turned 180 degrees from the direction of the put and was able to throw farther, because of the torque that developed as his body untwisted. Currently, shot-putters are trying to master a 360-degree turn because this should enable them to throw even farther. Similarly, the bent-arm pull in crawl stroke swimming is a radical departure from the straight-arm pull advocated until the 1950s.

We are now in a position to reverse the procedure outlined by Alley; biomechanical experts are leading the coaches, teachers, and athletes toward achieving better performance. The importance of their work to the performer is obvious—maximum achievement. The teacher/coach benefits, too, as he or she becomes more knowledgeable about efficient and effective ways to perform skills. Biomechanical experts have been responsible for equipment changes. Think how the tennis shoe has changed from one basic model (high top, canvas, heavy, all-purpose) to specialized designs and weights for specific purposes. Contrast pole vaulting using the bamboo poles of bygone days with the current flexible fiberglass poles; biomechanical experts were responsible for educating both performers and coaches so well that the former pole vaulting world record (which stood for years) now is attainable by many high school vaulters. Other professionals—rehabilitation specialists, engineers, aerospace workers—use the results of biomechanical research as well. Thus, the biomechanical expert is of importance both in fundamental research and in analysis of psychomotor performance.

LEARNING ABOUT BIOMECHANICS

Courses that most schools require for physical educators are briefly described here.

Algebra and Trigonometry. Many colleges expect physical education majors to have a basic knowledge in mathematics. This ordinarily means a high school course in both algebra and trigonometry. It is difficult to relate the physical principles of motion, angle of force, and pull of gravity to the body without at least a cursory knowledge of these two subjects. If not taken in high school, introductory college courses in these areas are often required.

Physics. A high school physics course is the minimum for a physical educator; it is often required in college.

Human Anatomy. This course was described in Chapter 6. It is logical to expect students to have an understanding of body structure before they can understand how the body moves.

Anatomical Kinesiology. This course follows the course in human anatomy; it provides an analysis of body structures as psychomotor movements are performed.

Mechanical Kinesiology (or **Biomechanics**). Following the anatomical studies mentioned above, biomechanics integrates the principles of physics into the analysis of psychomotor skill performance. A typical college course includes these units, as exemplified by Kreighbaum and Barthels' (1981) text: fundamental mechanical concepts; forces of human movement; general properties of the human body; mechanics of musculoskeletal structure; structural-functional relationships; biomechanical aspects of fitness activities and exercises; balance, equilibrium, and stability; principles of projectile motion; body rotation; timing of segmental rotation; movement in water; mechanical analysis of activities.

Physiology and **Physiology of Exercise.** These courses, described in Chapter 6, are related to biomechanics because physiology affects body movement. For example, as you tire when running, your slower speed shortens the stride length, which in turn affects biomechanical efficiency.

BIOMECHANICS AND YOU

As you probably know, there are national standardized achievement tests for students in almost every school subject. The value of these tests is that they permit easy comparisons of achievement among groups in widely separated schools. In some cases, they provide the standards used for promotion. AAHPERD was asked to develop such a test for physical education. First, a committee developed a teacher's guide, *Knowledge and Understanding in Physical Education.* This guide was to be used in helping the teacher ascertain what concepts and facts should be taught. Then a test, the AAHPERD Knowledge Test, was developed. The questions were primarily from the biological and kinesiological areas.

Remember that knowing about kinesiological principles and performing them adequately are two vastly different things. One way to judge your ability is to analyze your performance while playing or when taking such tests as mentioned in Chapter 7. Your scores will be an indication of your performance in comparison with the various normed groups. Notice low scores or inadequate performance; they could merely indicate a lack of practice, but they could also indicate that you are violating some mechanical principle or principles.

Student Activities

1. In your school library, try to find the *biomechanical* periodicals listed in Table 3.2 (p. 17). If you have time, read one article in each periodical.
2. Observe someone performing a motor skill. Analyze the movement, listing specific actions in the proper sequence.
3. Complete this sequence of statements.
   Stranger: What do you do?
   You: I'm a kinesiologist.
   Stranger: Oh? What does a kinesiologist do?
4. Talk to one or more physics majors. See if they can use the principle of levers to explain how a person walks.

Statements for Class Discussion

1. The terms "physical educator," "coach," and "biomechanics expert" are synonymous.
2. Can you explain these statements from a kinesiological standpoint?
   a. The bigger you are, the harder you fall.
   b. Weightlifters are certainly not double-jointed.
   c. The taller you are, the faster you can run.

Bibliography

Adrian, M. 1970. Formation and organization of human motion. *JOPERD* 41 (May): 73.

Alley, L. 1966. Utilization of mechanics in physical education and athletics. *JOPERD* 37 (March): 67-70.

Barrett, K. 1971. The structure of movement tasks. *Quest* 15 (January): 22-30.

Broer, M. 1966. *Efficiency of human movement*. Philadelphia: W. B. Saunders Co.

Bunn, J. W. 1972. *Scientific principles of coaching*. Englewood Cliffs, N.J.: Prentice-Hall.

Carr, J. A. 1978. The biomechanical perspective. Pp. 94-130 in Rivenes, R., ed. *Foundations of physical education*. Boston: Houghton Mifflin Co.

Cooper, J. 1980. Biomechanics. *JOPERD* 51 (November-December): 43-44.

Dyson, G. H. 1964. *Mechanics of athletics*. London: University of London Press.

Groves, R. 1971. Of coaches and researchers. *The Physical Educator* 34 (March): 15-16.

Johnson, W. O. 1977. This strange and perilous joint. *Sports Illustrated* 44 (October 24): 84-88.

Kreighbaum, E., and Barthels, K. 1981. *Biomechanics*. Minneapolis: Burgess Publ. Co.

Lay, K. 1971. Knowledge and understanding in physical education: Identifying the body of knowledge. *JOPERD* 42 (January): 21.

Lawther, J. 1966. Directing motor skill learning. *Quest* 6 (May): 68-76.

Luttgens, K., *et al*. 1980. Guidelines and standards for undergraduate kinesiology. *JOPERD* 51 (February): 19-21.

McCarthy, J. 1971. Form or performance for evaluation. *Minnesota JOHPE* (Fall): 21.

Moore, K. 1977. Gideon Ariel and his magic machine. *Sports Illustrated* 44 (August 22): 52-60.

Shornik, M. 1973. The magnificent obsession. *Sports Illustrated* 38 (April 30): 32.

Tanner, P., and Barrett, K. 1975. Movement education: What does it mean? *JOPERD* 46 (April): 19-20.

Verscoth, A. 1980. Tall story in skiing . . . boot that extends to the knee. *Sports Illustrated* 53 (December 22): 94.

chapter 10

Sociological Foundations of Physical Education

INTRODUCTION

Sport sociology is the subject of the final chapter in our discussion of the body of knowledge in physical education. This is appropriate because sport sociology involves a knowledge of physiological development, psychomotor learning, sport psychology, and biomechanics. This chapter will attempt to interrelate different issues about which physical educators must become familiar.

As Fraleigh has pointed out (Chapter 5), you must understand how physical education helps society by: (1) conferring survival benefits, (2) perpetuating certain cultural elements, (3) providing a medium for social mobility or rigidity, (4) objectifying, maintaining, or destroying prescribed relationships between individuals and institutions, and (5) providing a medium for persons of divergent background. To illustrate these points, this chapter begins with concepts, definitions, and examples of issues in sport sociology. The historical background of this area leads to a discussion of current sport issues in American life. Specific courses are described, with the chapter culminating in suggestions for self-assessment of your interest in sport sociology.

CONCEPTS TO BE GAINED FROM THIS CHAPTER

When you have mastered the material in this chapter, you will be able to demonstrate comprehension of these concepts:

1. Sport sociology includes the physiological, psychological, and biomechanical foundations of physical education while considering the effect of sport and physical activity on individuals, groups, and society.
2. Participation in sport is assumed to have eight distinctive values.
3. In order to discuss sport in American life intelligently, physical educators should be aware of how sports relate to these areas: youth, women, colleges, professionals, media, race, religion, business, fitness, and international competition.

DEFINITIONS

The following terms are pertinent to an understanding of sport sociology.

1. *Play*—Activity that is free, stands apart from ordinary life, and is serious to the player. The best example is the spontaneous play of children (Huizinga 1950, p. 10).
2. *Game*—An activity that contains the element of play, but in which the goals for participating originate outside the game itself. Rules are followed, and a winner is declared (Leonard 1980, p. 12).
3. *Sport*—Special types of games that require physical competition, follow prescribed rules, and have either intrinsic or extrinsic rewards (Leonard 1980, pp. 12-13).
4. *Sport sociology*—The scientific study of social structures and social processes in the world of sport (Leonard 1980, p. 15).
5. *Political influence*—Issues relating to the impact of local and national governments upon the lives of citizens. Examples are regulations that married high school students are ineligible to compete in athletics or that all students must take physical education. Many of you live in or near a community that has a public swimming pool or a professional football or baseball stadium. It was a political decision to tax citizens to pay for these and similar facilities.
6. *Social influence*—Issues relating to the impact of peers and society upon the lives of citizens. Have you experienced the community spirit within the squad, the student body, or the town when a basketball team wins a state championship? What about the influence that sports have on religion, and vice versa? Did you realize that "blue laws" formerly forbade the playing of sports on Sunday? Are you familiar with the Athletes in Action teams that tour the United States?
7. *Economic influence*—Issues relating to the impact of money and business upon the lives of citizens. Examples are the rise of tourism because of local sporting events, the millionaire status of certain professional athletes, school budgets for athletics.

HISTORICAL BACKGROUND OF SPORT

From the beginning of time, physical prowess was an economic, political, and social force. The person who could provide food for self and family was able to survive. As the fittest survived, tribes were formed. The tribes with the strongest and most cunning members took land from weaker tribes. As more land was accumulated, greater political, social, and economic pressures were felt. Societies grew, and eventually physical recreation evolved. Activities that were formerly utilized for protection and for food-gathering (e.g., running and throwing a spear) became focal points for social interaction (e.g., foot races and javelin throwing). The Olympics in Greece and the knighthood contests in medieval England are prime examples of such adaptations. As these contests attracted spectators, societies were affected economically as well as socially. Then, as now, sport and games affected many people in many ways.

Unfortunately, the effects of sport on people and societies, and the effect of society upon sport, were not considered a worthy area for study and research until recent years. Until then, the glowing testimonials of prominent people who attributed their success to athletic competition were enough to convince society that sport was valuable. Early sport sociologists, such as Huizinga and Caillois, provided the foundation for serious research in the United States. Kenyon and Loy's 1965 article, "Toward a Sociology of Sport," marks the date after which American sport sociology has slowly emerged and developed into an academic specialty, even though the 1953 publication of *Sports in American Life* by Cozens and Stumpf was the first major American publication in the field. The list of issues mentioned later in this chapter attests to the wide variety of topics that are relevant to today's sport sociologists.

THE VALUES OF SPORT

Earlier chapters have summarized the importance of physiological development, psychomotor skills, sport psychology, and biomechanics to physical educators and to the public groups that permit and/or encourage participation in play, games, and sport. The result of such participation is very beneficial, according to many. After a thorough review of the literature, Edwards (1973, pp. 63-69) developed a list of seven dominant values attributed to sport participation. These are:

1. *Character building*—Development of desirable personality traits
2. *Discipline*—Development of obedience to authority
3. *Competition*—Preparation for later life, in which competition is the key to success (Note that competition does not necessarily include winning!)
4. *Physical fitness*—Development of healthy bodies
5. *Mental fitness*—Development of alert minds
6. *Religiosity*—Reinforcement of traditional religious beliefs
7. *Nationalism*—Development of pride in our country

To the above list may be added an eighth value, that of *socialization of individuals*. In this regard, what effect does physical activity (e.g., play, games, or sport) have on participants? Kenyon (1968, p. 33) reports that persons might learn particular roles in order to be involved with sport (e.g., sportsmanlike conduct), but that these are not necessarily the roles needed in later life (e.g., high moral character). Little evidence has been found to suggest that physical education programs facilitate socialization in either the specific or the general roles that we assume. Finally, Kenyon suggests that, when planned for, physical education could contribute to the socialization process. Stevenson (1975, p. 287) concludes that there is no valid evidence that participation in sport causes any verifiable socialization effects.

Some claim that athletics, because it calls for personal dedication and effort on the part of the participant, will contribute more toward socialization than does physical education. However, racial problems between teammates offer proof that merely playing together will not cause mutual respect and friendship. Fights occur between teams and/or among spectators. Many individual studies relate physical activities to social development, antisocial behavior, personal-social adjustments, social mobility, social integration, aggression, and cooperation. The majority of these studies do show positive correlations when comparing athletic or physical education groups to nonathletic or nonphysical education groups, yet a cause-effect relationship is not indicated. In fact, two authorities have stated that athletics might *not* be the way to develop character, cooperation, and other values (Ogilvie and Tutko 1971, p. 60).

What can we state with assurance about the value of sport? As we mentioned in Chapter 8, hard scientific evidence is lacking, but the following general statement is acceptable: "Sport environments can be constructed to meet the participants' needs, foster desirable behavior, and create a positive psychological influence" (Fabian *et al.* 1980, p. 39, citing articles by Devereux, Loy, and McPherson). Note that the benefits *may* accrue in certain instances, but that they are *not* automatic.

SPORT IN AMERICAN LIFE

As a physical educator you need to be aware of the current topics in American society because you will eventually have to render professional opinions and judgments. The more you learn about the issues, the more professional and objective your views will be.

Youth Sport Competition

"Athletics Are Linked to Child Abuse," "Winning Isn't Everything Nor Is It the Only Thing," and "Little League Lunacy" are but three of many articles that are critical of youth sport competition. As previously mentioned, most adults and participants believe that organized sport programs are great, but the comment, "Little League would be great if it weren't for the parents," is not humorous to many coaches and league administrators. Complaints about adults are specific— overorganization, strict rules, emphasis on winning a championship, and incidents of verbal and physical confrontations with officials, coaches, other parents, and even their own children. Sage (1978, p. 42) points out that "organized sport— from youth programs through the pros—has nothing at all to do with playfulness—fun, joy, self-satisfaction—but is, instead, a social agent for the deliberate socialization of people into acceptance of our most salient organization form (bureaucracy)." Sage's comment, derived after careful research, is believable now, but it probably would not have been believed in 1965.

Efforts are being made to solve the problems inherent in youth sport programs. Sport sociologists, physical educators, and parents who coach have shown that youth programs can be conducted in an educational manner. AAHPERD is a leader in this area, with their publication *Youth Sports Guide for Coaches and Parents.*

Specific programs to educate coaches (most of whom are not certified physical educators or coaches) are found in many U.S. and Canadian cities (see Zarebski and Moriarty 1978, Laurie and Corbin 1981).

Women and Sport

A most significant piece of social legislation with important economic and political overtones was made law in June 1972. A portion of the Education Amendment of 1972, more popularly called Title IX, relates specifically to physical education and athletics. In essence, the governing clause states that: "No person in the United States shall, on the basis of sex, be excluded from taking part in, be denied the benefits of, or be subjected to discrimination under any educational program or act receiving federal financial assistance." Since virtually all public and private schools receive federal aid in varying amounts, under current interpretations, they must comply with the provisions of Title IX or lose all federal funds. The practical implication is that there can be no discrimination on the basis of sex in any education program or act sponsored by a school district, college, or university.

Title IX makes specific demands in terms of health, physical education, and athletics. The following are examples of such requirements:

1. Health education classes may be separated by sex only in sessions dealing with human sexuality.
2. Physical education classes may be separated by sex only for contact sports. The key requirement is that all classes must be available to both sexes, just as are classes in mathematics and English. This will cause concern to some physical education teachers, who have the attitude that only girls should take dance class and that only boys should take touch football class.
3. Facilities and equipment must be equally available to members of both sexes. Gone are the days when boys' teams automatically got the gym during prime time. Alternating and compromising on the scheduled use of fields, courts, and gyms will be a common practice. Equipment must be comparable in kind, quantity, and quality.
4. Physical activities and athletic opportunities must be equally available to members of both sexes. It is the duty of physical educators and coaches to determine the interests and abilities of students and, insofar as the school can afford it, meet the needs of all students. Separate athletic teams are required if both men and women express sufficient interest. Opening teams to both sexes is not enough, as men would dominate many teams and the result would not effectively accommodate the interests and abilities of women. Contrary to common thought, schools are not required to offer identical programs for both sexes; neither do money expenditures have to be identical. But publicity, travel expenses, number and salary of coaches, athletic scholarships, athletic training services—the items necessary to develop a total athletic program for men and women—must be comparable.

As you undoubtedly know, Title IX, with its accompanying social attitude change, has fostered drastic revisions in female athletic programs at all levels. For example (National Federation . . . 1980, Terp 1981, Wood 1980):

1. Between 1971 and 1978, there was a 600 percent increase in female participation in high school athletics, and a 250 percent increase in female participation in college athletics.
2. Females (after court decisions) are now permitted to play on all youth teams (e.g., baseball, football).
3. The number of women tennis players has increased from 3 million to 11 million since 1970; of women golfers, from 0.5 million to 5 million.
4. One-third of all joggers are female; in 1970, there were too few to count.
5. The number of female soccer players has increased 750 percent since 1975.
6. Over 700 women finished the 1981 Boston Marathon.
7. The women's share of the budgets in big-time college athletic programs has increased from 2.1 percent in 1973 to 14.3 percent in 1980.

Currently, a bitter struggle is occurring for control of women's collegiate athletics. The women's organization (AIAW) believes that the male-oriented and male-dominated groups (NCAA and NAIA) are interested in controlling the entire athletic program for budgetary rather than educational reasons. For example: it is desirable to have female coaches for women's teams, but Parkhouse and Holmen report that, although the number of collegiate coaching positions increased 37 percent between 1974 and 1979, the percentage of women employed in those positions decreased. In addition, the total number of female head coaches actually declined by 209 percent. Another point is that there is still a great discrepancy between the smaller amount of money spent by schools and colleges on female athletic programs and the larger expenditures for male athletes. These are but two reasons why the AIAW believes that a women's organization is the logical organization for control of athletics.

No doubt some years will pass before true equality of opportunity becomes a reality. Title IX is currently being attacked in the courts, but even if it is altered somewhat, the social climate in the United States is such that the gains attained by female sport participants will remain. Title IX is a good illustration of how sport is interrelated with the political, social, and economic areas, and how sport influences society, and vice versa.

College Athletics

While Title IX pressures and the NCAA/NAIA/AIAW struggle relate to male-female concerns, college athletics has other problems. Because it exists (in theory) for educational reasons, it is thought that individual athletes should be students first and athletes second. There is evidence that, at least in the male "pressure" sports, this theory is not supported in real life. For example, Burwell (1979, p. 21) points out that only 33 percent of the black athletes and 75 percent of the white athletes in the Southwestern Conference received their undergraduate degrees. Underwood (1980) talked about the "Student-Athlete Hoax," which involved falsifying transcripts and academic cheating. Revelations about a basketball fix involving point-shaving (i.e., reducing the margin of winning) were made public in 1981. Overshadowing all is the financial crunch; "Sports Programs' Costs Lead to College's Financial Disaster," warns one article (Middleton 1980). The problems are real, and college athletics will continue to be attacked.

Professional Athletics

Interest in professional sport is intense, perhaps because it receives so much attention from the media. Astronomical salaries, brought on in part by the rights of players to become free agents, have made millionaires of even average players. In 1980, the average professional basketball player received $180,000, an NFL player, $78,650, and a baseball player, $150,000. According to Kuhn, the average baseball player will probably receive about $320,000 by 1984 (Kaplan 1981). Despite these salaries, players claim that the owners are getting rich at players' expense, and both football and baseball players have called strikes to emphasize their demands. The average fan, who directly or indirectly pays the salaries, generally sides with the owners, as the quoted salary figures are so very high when compared to the salary of the average worker.

Race

Of interest to players, owners, and sport sociologists is the racial composition of teams, especially the professional ones. The percentage of black players has consistently risen over the years and currently approaches 35 percent in baseball, 45 percent in football, and 75 percent in basketball. Teams that have black leaders (head coaches and managers) are relatively few. Other areas of discrimination, according to some, are the stacking of black players in certain positions and in salary differentials. Owners worry about whether racial imbalance will help or hinder gate receipts, while players complain about the racial favoritism shown by the coach, manager, or owner.

Media

The impact of the mass media has always been a social and political influence on American sport. Recently, however, it has been the most dominant economic factor for some particular sports. Publicity from radio, television, newspapers, and magazines is the primary source of sports information for most of us.

Public interest in sporting events has, for dozens of years, caused newspapers to devote more space to this topic than to any others. Many believe that media coverage is responsible for recent dramatic increases in sports interest on the part of the American public. Bowling and tennis are prime examples. The Billie Jean King-Bobby Riggs match is said to have been the single most important factor behind the tennis boom, but without television, radio, and press, it would have been of no more significance than many similar matches played between men and women over the past years.

According to Leonard (1980, pp. 268-273), the economic impact of television on American sport is tremendous. The amount spent by networks (estimated at $1 billion in 1980) or the amount received by college and professional teams ($200 million in 1978) often means the difference between profit and loss. In turn, television has caused games to be rescheduled, rules to be altered, and franchises to be bought and sold.

Business

It is obvious to most people that sport is related closely to big business. In addition to their high salaries, players receive money to wear and to endorse products; owners buy and sell franchises (seemingly making money with each transaction); fans pay higher admission prices each year; prize money for winners increases; elaborate stadiums are built; ski areas suffer when lack of snow cuts their attendance. Sport sociologists note that expenditures for sporting goods increase every year, and sport businesses can be found in every city and town in the United States. Virtually every sport shows annual participation increases, which translate into jobs for many and enjoyment for all.

Religion

Religious groups abound in American society, and this force is and has been an influence on sport. Despite what you may infer from contemporary newspaper reports, the early Olympic Games were held to honor Greek gods; because the gods were thought to help the competitors, sacrificial altars were part of these early athletic contest sites. During the golden age of Greece, the mind-body-spirit triangle was depicted as being essential to the development of the whole person. In later years, the goals of organized religion were generally incompatible with those of sport. The Roman Catholic church eventually forbade the playing of the Olympics. The people did participate in recreational pursuits, but since these took time from the study of spiritual matters, the church was not at all supportive.

In early colonial America, the Puritans were concerned with hard work and were opposed to frivolous play. In spite of these conflicts, many early American churches realized that there was more to life than the cultivation of the spirit. Gyms and playgrounds built by churches were often publicly used. Turnverein halls were (and still are) sport centers supported by religious institutions. Perhaps the best-known group emphasizing the dual role of sports and spiritual needs today is the YMCA/YWCA. To attract young men to their religious program, the YMCA deliberately fostered sport participation. In the 1880s, it became so involved in providing facilities and leadership in physical activities that it was among the first members of the Amateur Athletic Union. Springfield College, a prominent Massachusetts institution that still trains physical education teachers today, began as a YMCA teacher-training institution. Today Ys across the country are providing both facilities and physical activities.

It is most likely that you have been exposed to a more evangelistic interrelationship of athletics and religion than the low-key YMCA. Incorporating Christianity and athletics is a primary purpose of both the Fellowship of Christian Athletes and a traveling group called Athletes in Action. Fellowship of Christian Athlete groups are organized on both high school and college levels. They sponsor workshops and summer camps with the purpose of bringing school athletes and professional athletes together in a Christian atmosphere. A different technique is followed by Athletes in Action. Their teams travel across the country, playing local teams in regulation games. During half time or intermissions, athletes give their witness to the relationship between athletics and Christianity. There is no doubt that religion will continue to make use of sports to influence American society.

Fitness

Exercise has also been used as an economic force. The famous Canadian 5BX (five basic exercises) program was devised by a physical educator in response to the Canadian Air Force's request for a quick, daily exercise regime designed to reduce the coronary problems of pilots. The Canadian Air Force approached this from an economic point of view. Too many pilots were suffering from heart problems in their early forties after the Air Force had spent thousands of dollars training them. Adult physical fitness programs also became very popular in the United States when the 5BX program was published.

Many companies now promote physical fitness and recreation programs for their employees. For example, the Firestone Rubber Company owns a country club used solely by employees. Increased productivity and less employee turnover are thought to result from these measures. The President's Council on Physical Fitness and Sports promotes the fitness programs conducted for business employees. National conferences are held by the American Association of Fitness Directors in Business and Industry (AAFDBI), at which professional fitness leaders discuss issues of common concern to the over 500 companies and several thousand individual members.

International Competition

The earliest accounts of athletics had a political flavor; they were contests between tribes or persons, between city-states in Greece, and between nations in the Olympic contests. Early societies had to stress physical abilities to survive; later, militaristic purposes and international esteem became prime reasons for athletics. Today we see physical activity as having extreme political purposes in some countries. The ultimate in physical activity for military purposes was found in the Hitler Youth Movement of the 1930s, culminating in what Hitler thought would be a Nazi triumph in the 1936 Olympics. Currently, in China, the U.S.S.R., and East Germany, personal fitness is viewed as a duty to the state. These and many other countries support national touring teams in several sports. Many persons look upon international sport triumphs as an indication that a certain political ideology is superior to all others. This nationalistic flavor (seen at its most dramatic in the opening parade and medal ceremonies of the Olympics) is deplored by some, but is a source of pride for many.

International sport has long been regarded as a means whereby athletes can compete in a friendly atmosphere, free of hatreds and prejudices; even a slight knowledge of the facts will indicate that this simply is untrue. For example, consider the question of amateurism. Americans accuse the Russians of permitting professionals to compete on their teams, because many of the Russian athletes train the year round and have a state job to support themselves and their families. But the Russians are unimpressed with the American view of granting athletic scholarships. If the scholarships are given for athletic ability and are worth thousands of dollars in tuition, room, and board, the Russians ask, "Just what is an amateur?"

All the nations of the world, and especially the small ones, use sport as a vehicle to gain international respect and fame. The success of the Ethiopian distance runners in recent Olympics has done a great deal to focus world attention on that country. Asia is considered a continent of poverty, overpopulation, and unrest. Yet every four years the Asian Games are held, and the host country spends millions to build beautiful facilities to impress the visiting athletes and spectators. The Pan-American Games since 1971 have seen "little" Cuba battle "giant" U.S.A. in the quest for gold medals. The British Empire Games and the European Championships are supposedly held for sporting reasons—but political use is made of the results.

Finally, the Olympics offer clear proof of the political problems inherent in competition. The number of serious arguments before, during, and after the Games staggers the senses of most sport-persons. Hitler's snubbing of Jesse Owens in the 1936 Olympics is well known; the 1968 Summer Olympics in Mexico City gave blacks from the United States the opportunity to turn the attention of the world to their feelings. In 1972, South Africa was not allowed to compete because several nations objected to its racial policies. The murders of Jewish athletes in Munich was an outrage viewed by millions on television. The 1976 Games in Montreal saw the Republic of China (Taiwan) withdraw because they could not use their official name; nearly all the South African nations boycotted the Games because New Zealand was participating. Until 1980, most Americans felt that international sport and politics were unrelated, yet the great majority of Americans supported President Carter's boycott of the Moscow Games. Is it any wonder that international sport, and especially the Olympics, are losing their aura of prestige as a vehicle for goodwill and understanding?

Summary

To become aware of the political, social, and economic forces acting upon our body of knowledge means that you must be aware of the total environment in which you live. A current issue on many campuses concerns whether athletic programs should be financed by all students through a required fee or financed out of general funds by those who wish to pay. At one major school, the student body president (a graduate student in physical education) believed that it should be voluntary. The athletic department disagreed. What is your stand? On what educational, political, social, and economic principles do you base your decision?

LEARNING ABOUT SPORT SOCIOLOGY

Customarily, all physical educators must take general education courses in the social sciences. Quite often you can select the courses. Logical choices are:

Political Science. This subject is the study of government and politics, its structure and policies. In nearly every school there is an introductory political science course. Material covered in this course represents the very minimum that a physical educator should know.

Sociology. This subject is defined as the scientific study of human social behavior and of the organization and function of groups. An introductory course such as "Principles of Sociology" or "Social Problems" represents the minimum preparation for a physical education major.

Economics. Courses in this discipline enable a physical educator to become familiar with such economic problems as population growth, income, employment, governmental budgets, and allocation of resources. Courses entitled "Principles of Economics" or "Economic Problems" should certainly be taken.

Sport Sociology. This is the basic course for physical educators. A typical text (Leonard 1980) contains the following chapters: Brief History of Social Organizations, Culture, Socialization, Social Deviance, Social Stratification, Blacks in Sport, Women in Sport, Small Groups, Economics and Politics, Mass Media, Collective Behavior and Social Change.

SPORT SOCIOLOGY AND YOU

There are no published tests that can be used by physical educators to assess their current status regarding knowledge of political, social, and economic forces. But you might reach a subjective judgment by answering these questions:

1. How much of the sports page in the daily paper do you regularly read? What other parts of the paper do you regularly read?
2. What other general sport periodicals (e.g., *Sports Illustrated, Women Sports, Sport,* sport sections of *Newsweek*) do you regularly read?
3. What specific sport periodicals (e.g., *Mentor, Coach and Athlete, Scholastic Coach, Athletic Journal, Swimming World, Modern Gymnast*) do you regularly read?
4. What have you read about the political, social, and economic aspects of sport?
5. How did you enjoy the Sport Sociology course?

Student Activities

1. In your school library, try to find the *sociological* periodicals listed in Table 3.2 (p. 17). If you have time, read one article in each periodical.
2. Visit one of the following situations: youth team workout, junior high girls' team workout, adult fitness workout at the YMCA (or similar group), Athletes in Action game; college team workout. Judging from what you have observed, what are the benefits of this activity to the participant? To society?

Statements for Class Discussion

1. Sports offer a person the best way to rise from the ghetto.
2. The changes being made because of Title IX are long overdue.
3. Title IX is a great idea, but it should be implemented more slowly.

Bibliography

Caillois, R. 1961. *Man, play, and games*. New York: Free Press.

Cozens, F., and Stumpf, F. 1953. *Sports in American life*. Chicago: University of Chicago Press.

Edwards, H. 1973. *Sociology of sport*. Homewood, Ill.: Dorsey Press.

Fabian, L., Ross, M., and Harwick, B. 1980. Every player wins in recreational sports. *JOPERD* 51 (November-December): 29-31.

Freischlag, J. 1980. Practical applications from sport sociology. *JOPERD* 51 (February): 36.

Huizinga, J. 1950. *Homo ludens—A study of the play element in culture*. Boston: Beacon Press.

Kenyon, G. 1968. Sociological considerations. *JOPERD* 39 (November-December): 31-33.

Kenyon, G., and Loy, J. 1965. Toward a sociology of sport. *JOPERD* 36 (May): 24.

Leonard, W. 1980. *A sociological perspective of sport*. Minneapolis: Burgess Publ. Co.

Loy, J. 1972. Case for the sociology of sport. *JOPERD* 43 (June): 50.

————. et al. 1980. The emergence and development of the sociology of sport as an academic specialty. *Research Quarterly for Exercise and Sport* 51 (March): 91-109.

Michener, J. 1976. *Sports in America*. New York: Random House.

National Federation of State High School Associations. 1980. *Interscholastic sports participation*. Kansas City, Mo.: The Association.

Ogilvie, B., and Tutko, T. 1971. Sport: If you want to build character, try something else. *Psychology Today* 5 (October): 61-63.

Sage, G. H. 1978. American values and sport: Formation of a bureaucratic personality. *JOPERD* 49 (October): 42-44.

Stevenson, C. 1975. Socialization effects of participation in sport: A critical review of the research. *Research Quarterly for Exercise and Sport* 46 (December): 287-301.

Tutko, T., and Bruns, W. 1976. *Winning is everything and other American myths*. New York: Macmillan.

Wilkerson, M., and Dodder, R. 1979. What does sport do for people? *JOPERD* 50 (February): 50-51.

BUSINESS AND MEDIA

Buckley, T. 1973. Business is a front seat for today's Super Bowl. *The New York Times* (January 14): 1.

Carol, J. 1973. TV talk. *Sports Illustrated* 39 (April 9): 9.

Chandler, J. 1977. TV and sports. *Psychology Today* 10 (April): 64-76.

Johnson, W. O. 1980. This could be the last resort. *Sports Illustrated* 53 (December 15): 78-82.

Kennedy, R. 1977. Who are these guys? *Sports Illustrated* 44 (January 31): 50-58.

Looney, D. 1976. The start of a chain reaction. *Sports Illustrated* 44 (February 16): 18-20.

Middleton, L. 1979. The cable connection. *Chronicle of Higher Education* (December 3): 6-7.

Reed, J. D. 1974. The Louisiana purchase. *Sports Illustrated* 40 (July 22): 66-80.

Seybold, D. 1981. Jim McKay: TV and the amateur athlete today. *Coach and Athlete* 43 (May-June): 13-17.

COLLEGE ATHLETICS

Brown, G. 1972. Jeepers! Peepers is in charge now. *Sports Illustrated* 37 (October 23): 40-49.

Burwell, B. 1979. Scholarship athletes: Is there life after football? *Chronicle of Higher Education* (November 26): 21-22.

Hill, H. 1981. How I put the fix in. *Sports Illustrated* 48 (February 16): 14-21.

Kennedy, R. 1974. A case in point. *Sports Illustrated* 40 (June 10): 87-100; (June 17): 24-30.

Middleton, L. 1980. Sports programs' costs lead colleges to financial disaster, report charges. *Chronicle of Higher Education* (June 16): 15.

Underwood, J. 1980. The writing is on the wall. *Sports Illustrated* 47 (May 19): 36-72.

INTERNATIONAL SPORTS

Carry, P. 1974. Going to bat for Taiwan. *Sports Illustrated* 41 (August 19): 64-74.
Johnson, W. 1972. Faces on a new China scroll. *Sports Illustrated* 39 (September 24): 82-86; (October 2): 43-46.
Kennedy, R. 1975. The man who stood sports on its head. *Sports Illustrated* 42 (April 28): 22-24.
Kusserow, J. 1971. Games as a medium for world understanding. *JOPERD* 42 (January): 46.
Lucas, J. 1973. Open letter to Lord Killanin. *JOPERD* 44 (February): 8-10.
Maetozao, M., and Kim, D. 1979. Physical education and sport in the Soviet Union. *The Physical Educator* 36 (March): 39-44.
Mechikoff, R. 1980. The political nature of the Montreal Olympiad. *The Physical Educator* 37 (October): 147-150.
Rahrig, D. 1970. Race and races: American participation in the Olympic Games of 1936 and 1968. *The Physical Educator* 27 (March): 58.

PROFESSIONAL SPORTS

Briner, B. 1973. Making sport of us all. *Sports Illustrated* 39 (December 10): 36.
Brown, R. 1973. The Black gladiator—the major force in modern American sport. *NCPEAM Proceedings*: 43-50.
Eitzen, S., and Yetman, N. 1977. Immune from racism? *Civil Rights Digest* 9 (Winter): 3-13.
Kaplan, J. 1981. Is there a ceiling? *Sports Illustrated* 48 (January 5): 35-38.
Kennedy, R., and Williamson, N. 1978. Money and sports. *Sports Illustrated* 45 (July 31): 34-50.
Lombardo, B. 1978. The Harlem Globetrotters and the perpetuation of the Black stereotype. *The Physical Educator* 35 (May): 60-63.

RELIGION

Deford, F. 1976. Religion in sport. *Sports Illustrated* 44 (April 19): 88-102; (April 26): 64-69; (May 3): 42-60.

WOMEN AND SPORT

Gilbert, B., and Williamson, N. 1973. Sport is unfair to women. *Sports Illustrated* 40 (May 28): 88-98; (June 6): 44-54; (June 13): 59-65.
———— and ————. 1974. Women in sport: A progress report. *Sports Illustrated* 41 (July 29): 27-31.
Kaplan, J. 1979. *Women and sports.* New York: The Viking Press.
Parkhouse, B., and Holmen, M. G. [Date unknown.] Multivariate considerations in the selection of coaches for female athletes. *Update.*
Pennington, J., and Schumacher, S. 1980. Title IX: Perceptions and implications. *Update* (November): 4.
Terp, C. 1981. Women in sports. *Christian Science Monitor* (May 19-22). Four-part series.
Wood, P. S. 1980. Female athletes: They've come a long way, baby. *The New York Times Magazine* (May 18): 31.

YOUTH SPORTS

Bunker, L. 1981. Elementary physical education and youth sport. *JOPERD* 52 (February): 27.
Dubois, P. 1980. Competition in youth sports: Process or product? *The Physical Educator* 37 (October): 151-154.

Gould, D. 1981. Role of the physical educator in non-school youth sports. *The Physical Educator* 38 (May): 99-104.

Laurie, D., and Corbin, C. 1981. Parental attitudes concerning modifications in baseball for young children. *The Physical Educator* 38 (May): 105-109.

Simon, J. 1979. America's attitude toward youth sports. *The Physical Educator* 36 (December): 186-190.

Smoll, F., and Smith, R. 1981. Preparation of youth sport coaches: An educational application of sport psychology. *The Physical Educator* 38 (May): 85-98.

Zarebski, J., and Moriarty, D. 1978. SIR/CAR studies longitudinal changes in Little League baseball and implications for youth sports. *Update* (December): 13.

chapter **11**

Careers in Physical Education

INTRODUCTION

For decades, virtually all physical education majors in the United States have been prepared as teachers. In some cases, their professional preparation program was designed for teaching specialties such as elementary or secondary school physical education, coaching, or adapted physical education. Other programs prepared generalists—those who could teach health as well as physical education and coach several sports. Whether generalists or specialists, graduates were prepared to function only in a school situation.

A teacher surplus, combined with the societal trends described below, occurred in the early 1970s. Because physical educators were unable to obtain jobs for which they were trained, certain colleges began to develop so-called alternative programs, i.e., programs in which teacher certification was not received. In some cases, these alternative programs were nothing more than the same curriculum in physical education minus education courses and student teaching. Other physical education departments, being more cognizant of the needs of society, developed specific courses and curricula to meet certain identifiable jobs such as physical fitness specialist, preschool physical education teacher, aquatic administrator, and dance specialist.

Our view is that numerous jobs are needed in society that physical educators can and should do, and that teaching and coaching represent only one of six career categories. Thus, there are no alternative careers, only a number of viable options. This chapter will establish the reasons why professional preparation programs have broadened; it will present six major career categories and more than 30 specific job titles for which a background in physical education is desirable and even essential. Then, because there are great misconceptions concerning the similarities between physical education, health education, and recreation, the chapter will conclude with a discussion of the relationship among these three disciplines.

CONCEPTS TO BE GAINED FROM THIS CHAPTER

When you have mastered the material in this chapter, you will be able to demonstrate comprehension of these concepts:

1. Societal changes, such as the supply and demand for teachers, population characteristics, personal income expenditures, work-week adjustments, and national participation in sport and exercise, call for a revision of the traditional practice of preparing all physical educators as teachers.
2. There are six distinct categories of sport and physical education careers.
3. The discipline of physical education has a close relationship to the disciplines of health and recreation, but professional preparation programs in each are different.

SOCIETAL TRENDS

Because education curricula both reflect the past and prepare for the future, changes in society will always affect curricula. The past decade has seen major societal effects upon physical education, as on other disciplines.

Beginning in the early 1970s, the age of the population has undergone major revisions because the birth rate has declined and longevity has increased. These changes have resulted in a continually higher average age of the population. An improved level of fitness, both youth and adult, is evidence of increased participation in all manner of physical activity and exercise. The mobility of citizens, shown in sizeable population decreases in the Northeast and upper Midwest and great increases in the Sun Belt states, has caused school and government officials severe facility and personnel problems.

Economic changes have likewise affected physical education and sport. The tax base changes rapidly, with state and federal government support dependent to a large extent upon political considerations. Passage of social legislation (Title IX, affirmative action, etc.) has had significant financial implications. Rising personal income (fueled in part by two-salary households) has resulted in more spendable dollars; much of this is spent on sport-related activities. Finally, the work week has been shortened or altered, as four ten-hour work days are becoming common; this permits more leisure time for recreational pursuits.

What have these changes meant for careers in physical activity and sport? Consider the following:

Teaching and Coaching. Preschool physical education programs are found in numerous day-care centers. Taxpayer objections have caused some school districts to reduce the number of physical education teachers, yet the rise in sports participation by girls and women has effected an increase in the number of coaching jobs available. Youth sport programs have spawned numerous private swim and gymnastic schools, dance studios, and sport camps.

Fitness, Rehabilitation, and Therapy. At the upper end of the age spectrum, fitness and recreational leaders are to be found in senior citizen centers. In an effort to reduce employee health costs and turnover, corporations have developed exercise rooms and programs and have hired specialists. Local and state governments have likewise expanded their staffing for parks and recreational facilities. While therapy positions have not kept pace with the need, nevertheless, more and more therapists are being employed. Athletic trainers are becoming common in school systems. Physicians may specialize in sports medicine.

Sales and Administration. Scarcely a town or city in the United States is without a sporting goods store or at least a department in a general store. Would not a physical educator with a business background be the ideal person to own and/or operate such a business? Administrators and other business specialists are needed for the numerous sport schools, professional and private sport groups as mentioned above.

Performance and Communication. Professional leagues in soccer (both indoor and outdoor), women's softball, minor league football and basketball have arisen, along with expansion of the established leagues in football, basketball, ice hockey, and baseball. The tremendous public interest in sports and in the performers requires writers and sportscasters, sports information directors, and promotion specialists.

Careers in Sport and Physical Activity

There is no doubt that the opportunities for physical educators are greater now than ever before, but the ability to engage in a meaningful career depends upon educational preparation.

Table 11.1 summarizes six physical education and sport career categories, along with job titles and places of employment. All are highly appropriate for physical education majors, because they call for specialized education, which is part of our discipline. For the most part, these are full-time positions, or at least part-time opportunities to earn significant income. Hundreds of persons are employed in each of the jobs given, but the demand varies. Chapters 12-15 will discuss each of these career categories in more detail.

TABLE 11.1. CAREER OPPORTUNITIES IN PHYSICAL EDUCATION AND SPORT

CAREER CATEGORY/JOB TITLE	TYPICAL PLACES OF EMPLOYMENT
Teaching and Coaching	
1. Teacher	Schools: preschool through college Private groups: bowling alley, dance studio, golf club, gymnastics school, handball/racquetball club, swimming school, tennis center. Government: city recreation department Agency: YMCA, YWCA, Boys Clubs
2. Researcher/scholar	Schools: college and university Private: clinic, laboratory
3. Coach	Schools: junior high, high school, college Private groups: professional team

TABLE 11.1. (Continued)

CAREER CATEGORY/JOB TITLE	TYPICAL PLACES OF EMPLOYMENT
Fitness, Rehabilitation, and Therapy	
4. Fitness leader	Schools: college Private groups: health spa, athletic club, corporation Government: city recreation department Agency: YMCA, YWCA
5. Exercise physiologist	Schools: college, medical school Private groups: clinic, laboratory, medical equipment manufacturer
6. Physician (sports medicine)	Schools: college Private groups: clinic, hospital, professional team
7. Athletic trainer	Schools: college Private groups: clinic, professional team

8. Therapist
  a. Corrective
  b. Physical
  c. Dance
  d. Recreation
  e. Cardiac
	Schools: school district, college
	Private groups: clinic, hospital, institutions
	Government: institutions
	Agency: Easter Seal Society

9. Adapted physical education specialist	School: school district, college
Sales	
10. Owner/manager	Private groups: retail store, wholesale dealer, manufacturer
11. Salesperson	Private groups: retail store, wholesale dealer
12. Traveling sales representative	Private groups: wholesale dealer, manufacturer, book publisher
Management	
13. Owner	Private groups: athletic club, bowling alley, dance studio, figure salon, fitness center, golf course, gymnastic school, handball/racquetball club, health club, swim school, tennis center

14. Chief administrator
  a. General manager
  b. Athletic director
  c. Executive director
  d. Intramural director
  e. Recreation director
	Schools: college, athletic conference
	Private groups: professional team/league, touring group, corporation
	Government: city recreation department
	Agency: YMCA

15. Business administrator	Schools: college Private groups: professional team/league, touring group
16. Facility director	School: school district, college Private groups: professional team, sport center Government: city recreation department
Performance	
17. Professional athlete	Private groups: touring professional in golf, bowling, dance, ice skating, tennis, rodeo; team member in basketball, football, ice hockey, soccer, baseball
18. Official	Private groups: amateur (including school) and professional leagues
Communication	
19. Sports writer	Private groups: newspapers, magazines
20. Sports broadcaster	Private groups: radio and TV stations
21. Sports information director	School: college Private groups: professional team/league

THE RELATIONSHIP OF PHYSICAL EDUCATION TO HEALTH EDUCATION

Introduction

Health, a universal concern since the beginning of time, has traditionally been related to school physical education in the United States. In Chapter 4, we indicated that physical education was added to the school curriculum in the 1850s because of the value of "ten minutes of daily calisthenics." By 1890, health education was also a part of the curriculum, as every state required all students to attend at least one annual lecture on the "evils of alcohol and narcotics." As such courses as personal hygiene, human physiology, and sex education were added to the curriculum, the physical educator, who most likely had a college major in health and physical education, was asked to assume these additional teaching assignments. Many physical educators disliked these assignments, because they were unprepared to teach in a classroom.

Separation of Health From Physical Education

Since 1910, health educators have been attempting to separate the teaching of health from school physical education. They have emphasized that community health and school health are equally important aspects of their work, and that a total health program includes services and sound living practices as well as education. Unfortunately, most school health teachers, until the last ten years, were trained as physical education teachers. Very few had awareness of, let alone knowledge about, the numerous topics that should be taught in a good school health education curriculum. (Did your school health classes include such subjects as consumer health, dental health, drugs, human ecology, sex education, mental health, nutrition, personal health, prevention and control of disease, public and environmental health, safety education, and smoking? If so, your school probably employed a health education specialist.)

Since the early 1970s, most states have required teachers to earn majors in the areas in which they teach. Since four years is an inadequate time to educate specialists effectively in both physical education and health, the generalist health and physical education degree is seldom found in colleges these days.

Careers in Health

According to the National Health Council, there are more than 200 occupations in the health field, divided into these career categories:

Administrative, business, and clerical specialties
Clinical laboratory and technical services
Dental services
Dietetics and nutrition services
Environmental health
Health and medical research
Home care
Information and communication

Inhalation therapy
Library science
Medicine
Mental health
Nursing
Pharmacy
Physician's assistant
Public health
Rehabilitation
Social services
Speech and hearing
Vision care

Perhaps conspicuous by its absence is the teaching category. Actually, the teaching of health education is the job of many hundreds of persons. They are found most often in junior/middle schools, high schools, and colleges, and in the education divisions of government and other agencies. Health teachers are most apt to be members of the Association for the Advancement of Health Education (AAHE), which is one of the seven associations in AAHPERD. Health education majors do not consider themselves qualified to teach physical education—and they are convinced that, although the two areas are complementary, they are not the same.

THE RELATIONSHIP OF PHYSICAL EDUCATION TO RECREATION

Introduction

According to Buchanan (1977, p. 216), "recreation is the utilization of activities which are voluntarily selected and from which personal satisfaction is gained." Since the beginning of time, people have engaged in recreation after working hours, but it is only with the advent of labor-saving devices and with a higher standard of living that persons have found it necessary to become concerned with worthy use of leisure time.

In the early days in the United States, the Puritan work ethic discouraged use of leisure time in any way that was not church related. However, this attitude quickly gave way to the American love of games, sports, and dancing. What once was a necessity (hunting, fishing, farming) has become, for many, recreation. Thus, virtually every town and city has numerous groups and facilities where residents can participate in leisure activities. The societal trends cited earlier in this chapter ensure that recreation—and the need for trained persons to guide the activities—will continue to grow.

Separation of Recreation From Physical Education

To many people, recreation means playing games. As these people observe physical education classes where students do little except play, they conclude that there is no difference between recreation and physical education. As Buchanan (1977, p. 216) emphasizes, golf skills are sometimes learned in a physical education class or sometimes they are learned as the game is played during leisure time. Sometimes we have a trained teacher, at other times we teach ourselves or learn from peers. If the learning and using of physical skills is the only aspect considered, then indeed recreation and physical education are intertwined.

Recreationists emphasize that physical skills are only one aspect of a desirable recreation program, however, and assert that the organization and administration of a modern recreation program calls for much more than the psychomotor teaching skills learned by most physical educators. Unfortunately, it has been only in recent years that employers have grasped the philosophy that recreation is a broad spectrum of worthy leisure-time pursuits. Until then, employers hired physical education majors to lead recreation programs—and expected little more than well-organized athletic leagues.

Careers in Recreation

A complete listing of the many specific job titles in recreation is beyond the scope of this text. Table 11.2 summarizes the principal jobs found in seven major employer groups, and it will give you an overview of the opportunities in recreation.

The National Recreation and Park Association (NRPA) is the primary professional group to which any person in recreation should belong. There is also a recreation association within AAHPERD, but it has a smaller membership and is more limited in scope.

THREE SEPARATE DISCIPLINES

As has been noted, there are similarities among physical education, health, and recreation, the basic one being that all three are people-oriented. In addition, they are all concerned with the physical, social, and/or emotional health of people, especially as it concerns their fitness practices and attitudes. The differences among them are real, however—and no amount of tradition can refute this fact. Physical education and health have strong foundations in the sciences, while recreation leans more heavily on the social sciences. The jobs performed by workers in each of these disciplines are different, with recreation being much broader in scope. In this age of specialization, it is simply impossible to remain competent without continual education—and time limits the developing of expertise needed in different disciplines.

To say it yet another way, we believe that it is in your best interest to seek a career for which you have received the best possible education. You are, no doubt, interested in health, recreation, *and* physical education. In all probability, however, you will be more interested in one than the others. This is the area in which to major. Select a school that offers a strong major in the discipline of your choice. If the college you select offers excellent programs in two or three of the disciplines, so much the better; a few courses in each of the other disciplines will be valuable. If your career goal changes, do not be hesitant to change majors or colleges. The loss of a few credits and the slight additional expense will be offset by the education you receive and the expertise you will bring to your career.

TABLE 11.2. RECREATION EMPLOYERS AND JOB TITLES

EMPLOYING GROUP	EXAMPLES OF SPECIFIC JOB TITLES
Government Federal (Departments of Interior, Agriculture, Defense)	Park worker (manager, ranger, naturalist, historian, designer)
State (Department of Natural Resources, planning agency)	Land acquisition officer Conservation specialist
County	Interpretive specialist Recreation specialist Campground manager Outdoor recreation specialist Engineer Resource planner Administrator
City	Director of recreation Director of parks Recreation program supervisor Recreation specialist Community center director Sport specialist (aquatics, golf, etc.)
Armed forces	Recreation program supervisor Recreation specialist Sport specialist (aquatics, golf, etc.)
Schools	Community education director Community school director Intramural director College instructor
Industry	Recreation director Physical fitness specialist
Voluntary agencies (YMCA, Scouts, etc.)	Executive director Program director Camp director Aquatic specialist Outdoor recreation specialist Youth activity specialist
Hospitals and institutions	Therapeutic recreation specialist Geriatric specialist
Private groups	Tourist agent Leisure counselor Teaching professional (golf, tennis, racquetball, handball, aquatics)

Adapted from D. Buchanan, The relationship of physical education to recreation (Chap. 15 in R. D. and J. A. Clayton, *Concepts and careers in physical education* [Minneapolis: Burgess Publ. Co., 1977]), pp. 219-222; and from C. Jensen, *Recreation and leisure time careers* (Skokie, Ill.: VGM Career Horizons, 1976), pp. 79-94.

Student Activities

1. Using the categories given in Table 11.1, look in the Yellow Pages of your telephone book. How many of the categories are listed?
2. Think about sport careers in your home town. How many of the jobs listed in Table 11.1 were available?

3. Talk to a high school health and physical education teacher. Does he or she feel equally qualified in each discipline? If not, why not?
4. Obtain a program description of the recreation program in your home town. Contrast it with the physical education program which you experienced in high school. What are the differences?

Statements for Class Discussion

1. My career goal is _____ (one of the careers mentioned in Table 11.1) because _____ .
2. Health, physical education, and recreation have little in common and should be in separate college departments.

Bibliography

Annarino, A. 1979. Professional preparation: Riding a pendulum. *JOPERD* 50 (October): 18-20.

Bryant, J. 1979. The year 2001 A.D. and future careers in physical education. *The Physical Educator* 36 (December): 197-200.

Buchanan, D. 1977. The relationship of physical education to recreation. Chap. 15 in Clayton, R. D., and Clayton, J. A. *Concepts and careers in physical education.* Minneapolis: Burgess Publ. Co.

Clayton, R. D., and Clayton, J. A. [n.d.] No alternative careers in physical education. *Infusing career education into physical education and sport.* Reston, Va.: AAHPERD. Pp. 19-21.

Fried, D. H. 1979. Alternative career opportunities related to physical education. *JOPERD* 50 (January): 72.

Groves, R. 1979. Career options within the undergraduate major. *JOPERD* 50 (June): 84.

Jensen, C. 1976. *Recreation and leisure time careers.* Skokie, Ill.: VGM Career Horizons.

Lambert, C. 1978. That's not physical education—or is it? *JOPERD* 49 (February): 30-31.

———. 1980. What can I do besides teach? *JOPERD* 51 (November-December): 74-76.

———. 1980. What is physical education? *JOPERD* 51 (May): 27-28.

Reid, M., ed. 1979. Careers in leisure and recreation: A look at the potential. *Leisure Today* (April): 1-31.

Swofford, A. 1980. Alternatives to jock itch. *JOPERD* 51 (November-December): 13.

chapter 12

Teaching and Coaching

INTRODUCTION

Teaching physical education or coaching sport teams tends to be the professional goal of the majority of students who enter our discipline. In most cases, their goal is to work with school students; but there are more and more opportunities these days for teaching and coaching in out-of-school situations as well. Regardless of the student's age or the teaching site, physical educators and coaches must apply their knowledge of biological development, sport psychology, sport sociology, psychomotor learning, and biomechanical skills to their work.

This chapter will begin with a listing of concepts, followed by a description of how the body of knowledge relates to the basic purposes of teaching and coaching. Physical education teaching is then discussed, including definitions of terms and descriptions of several different teaching situations, both school and nonschool. A career in research and scholarly work is noted. Attention is then focused on coaching, beginning with definitions of appropriate terms. The extent of student participation in school athletics is discussed, and coaching opportunities in both school and professional situations are outlined. Duties, salaries, and job satisfactions of both teachers and coaches are presented. The college courses you will need to become a competent teacher or coach are described.

Organizations of interest to teachers and coaches are listed in Appendix A.

CONCEPTS TO BE GAINED FROM THIS CHAPTER

When you have mastered the material in this chapter, you will be able to demonstrate comprehension of these concepts:

1. The purposes of teaching physical education and/or coaching are directly related to the body of knowledge given in Chapters 5-10 of this text.
2. Numerous terms ("physical education," "educational athletics," "salary schedule," etc.) must be understood before you can seriously consider your future involvement in physical education or coaching.
3. The terms "physical educator" and "coach" are not synonymous. Although one person can possess the skills to perform both jobs competently, the goals, duties, and strategies used in each role are different.
4. At this point, teaching physical education is or is not an appropriate career goal for you. This concept is based on a tentative understanding of:
   a. The age level (e.g., preschool, K-6, etc.) at which you would or would not prefer to teach
   b. The qualities of a successful physical education teacher that you possess or lack
   c. The activity skills you will need to develop to conduct a varied physical education program.
5. At this point, coaching sports is or is not an appropriate career goal for you. This concept is based upon a tentative understanding of:
   a. The coaching skills you will need to develop
   b. The apprenticeship experience you will need to undergo
   c. How your personal goals fit into the roles expected of a coach.

BASIC PURPOSES OF TEACHING PHYSICAL EDUCATION AND COACHING ATHLETICS

In Chapter 5, the ideas of Fraleigh concerning the discipline of physical education were presented. Subsequent chapters (6-10) amplified the knowledge and understandings that compose our body of knowledge. Most people regard physical education as only a subject taught in school. We prefer that you think of physical education as a discipline, and that you realize that professional educators apply the body of knowledge in such a way that students will profit now and in later years. Consider how the purposes of school physical education relate to our body of knowledge. According to AAHPERD (1962), school physical education should:

1. Condition heart, lungs, muscles, and other organic systems to respond to increased demands by imposing progressively greater demands upon them
2. Help children learn to move skillfully and effectively, not only in exercise, games, sports, and dances, but also in all active life situations
3. Enrich understandings of voluntary movement and the ways in which individuals may organize their own movements to accomplish the significant purposes of their lives
4. Extend understanding of socially approved patterns of personal behavior, with particular reference to the interpersonal interactions of games and sports.

The purposes of coaching, at least for school athletics, relate directly to these AAHPERD statements. You may be surprised to realize that most nations of the world do not include athletics as part of their school programs. These countries do not feel that sponsorship of school teams will help them meet their educational goals. We believe differently; we organize all types of college, high school, junior high school, and elementary school teams. Most nations have local sports clubs or government-sponsored groups similar to our Little League baseball, age-group swimming, Biddy Basketball, and gymnastic clubs. We view athletics as educational in nature, designed to improve students in physical, social, and emotional areas. We believe that schools can do this better than out-of-school groups.

Coaches of age-group teams, even though these are outside the organized school structure, obstensibly have the same goals as are listed above. Professional coaches have a different goal—that of winning, which in turn attracts paying spectators so that the enterprise can remain solvent. Little attention is given to educational goals. Nevertheless, the facts and knowledges related to biological development, biomechanical skills, and sport psychology must be foremost in the minds of the coaches.

Comparing the purposes of school physical education and athletics with the material in Chapters 5-10 (as shown in Figure 12.1) brings to light a remarkable similarity. It is evident that, in order for physical educators and coaches to affect people's life, they must be concerned with the three domains that relate to all learning. Concepts and facts must be discovered and organized into a body of knowledge. Then professional teachers and coaches, who understand both the body of knowledge and effective teaching/coaching techniques, determine what and how persons should be guided. The purposes of physical education and school athletics (as cited above) must agree with the basic philosophy of society toward education. Society determines the ultimate goals of education and the role of sport in the United States, but professional physical educators and coaches determine the best way to achieve them.

PHYSICAL EDUCATION TEACHING

Definitions

There are many terms that you should understand before reading farther in this chapter; definitions are given below.

1. *Physical education*—A broad program consisting of individual sports, team sports, dance, aquatics, and exercises. This program may be conducted in the schools, agencies (YMCA), sport centers, etc.
2. *Specialty program*—The focus is devoted exclusively to one activity (e.g., gymnastics, swimming, dance). This program is usually conducted in a private business setting or as an independent aspect of an agency program.
3. *Required program*—Physical education classes taken because either the state law or the local school district requires it.

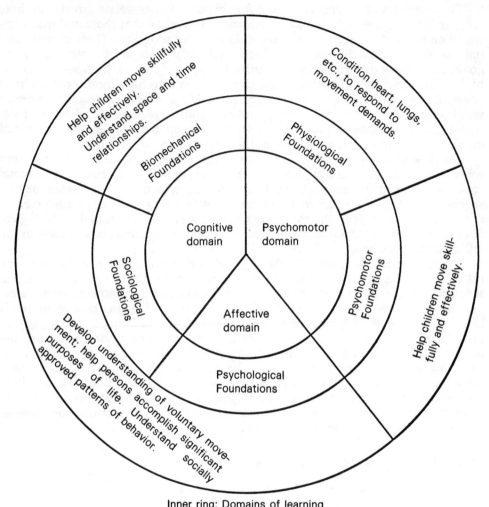

Inner ring: Domains of learning
Middle ring: Body of knowledge in physical education
Outer ring: Purposes of school physical education and athletics

FIGURE 12.1. Relationship of the body of knowledge to the purposes of school physical education and athletics.

4. *Elective program*—Students may elect to take physical education if they wish. The option usually is granted only to those in grades 10-12.
5. *Required elective program*—One in which students must take physical education, but may choose which activities they wish to learn.
6. *Teacher certification*—This refers to the State Department of Education requirements that you must meet to receive a license (or certificate) to teach. All teachers from kindergarten through high school level must be

certified by the state in which they teach. On successful completion of certain required courses, your college will verify to the state that you have met all requirements and should receive a certificate. Interestingly enough, there are no certification requirements to teach in four-year colleges; a college could (and sometimes does) hire persons without a college degree.

7. *Education courses*—Those courses that deal with teaching. They are offered by the Department of Education and generally involve principles of learning, growth and development, measurement and evaluation, and student teaching.

8. *Low-organized games*—These are sometimes called elementary games. Examples are tag, hopscotch, and rope jumping. The rules are simple and feature much action for many children. Basically, they are found in grades K-4 and are used both because the students learn rules and gain fitness and agility and because they are fun!

9. *Lead-up games*—These involve one or two skills of a highly organized game. For example, a basketball dribble relay is a lead-up game to basketball. Lead-up games are taught so that students may practice just one or two aspects of the more difficult game.

10. *Recess*—A period (usually twice a day for 15 minutes) when elementary school children are encouraged to go outside or to the gym, where they can play as they wish.

11. *Roll-out-the-ball program*—In such a program, the physical educator does no direct teaching, but merely takes attendance and then lets the students play. This type of program is universally condemned by physical education leaders, but, for one reason or another, it exists all over the United States. The lazy physical educator who uses this type of program is probably the chief culprit in convincing citizens that their child should take an "academic" course rather than a "play" course.

12. *Intramural*—The word means "within walls," according to the Latin from which it came. Intramural (not *inter*mural) activities are those events (sports, plays, debates, etc.) that occur within the walls of a school. For example, when one seventh-grade class challenges another class from the same school to a contest, it is an intramural contest.

13. *Probationary period*—During this time, teaching supervisors are attempting to evaluate your effectiveness as a teacher. A teacher can be released (i.e., dismissed from the job) if the teacher-effectiveness evaluations are unsatisfactory; this period lasts from one to six years.

14. *Tenure*—Status as a teacher, achieved after satisfactory probationary status. It means that the school district or institution agrees that you will continue to be employed for as long as you wish, except for serious reasons (e.g., immoral conduct).

15. *Salary schedule*—Salary figures agreed upon by the district and the teachers' association. The salary depends on your degrees and years of experience. Usually each year of experience means an increase in salary. In years past, salaries were set by negotiation between the superintendent and each teacher, but now salary schedules are found in most school

districts. A common misconception is that teachers in elementary schools are paid less than high school teachers. If there is a salary schedule, all teachers in that district, regardless of where they teach, are paid according to the agreed-upon figure and their position on the salary schedule.

TEACHING IN SCHOOLS

Physical education teachers are found in a number of school levels. The duties, responsibilities, employment conditions, and salaries at each level are different, as noted in the sections to follow.

Preschool Teaching

Currently, the great majority of physical education programs begin with kindergarten-age children, but there is a strong trend toward providing such programs for preschool children (ages three to five) as well. At this point, these programs are not usually part of the public or parochial school systems; however, since they provide a career opportunity for you, they will be considered here.

A child first learns through the senses. At about age three, children become interested in other people and things; they are beginning to experience socialization in various aspects of play—talking, singing, writing, etc. Motor movements (e.g., running, hopping) should be emphasized, both for their psychomotor value and for socialization purposes. "Ceaseless activity" (Werner 1975, p. 181) describes the behavior of children at this age. Gradually, psychomotor movements are directed toward organized group activities (tag, cops and robbers, hide and seek).

We all know that psychomotor development of children will occur with or without the help of a physical educator. So why is there a trend to provide such a specialist in nursery or other preschool settings? First, there is reason to believe that psychomotor skills must be developed if school instruction is to be of optimal benefit to the child. Balance, locomotion, and manipulative skill aid in drawing, letter formation, and playing in a group. Hand-eye and foot-eye coordination are useful in situations other than batting or kicking!

How are psychomotor skills best taught? Most of us learned through trial and error as we played around the home, but logic indicates that a specialist could teach skills better, quicker, and more correctly than would occur with aimless experimentation on the part of a three-year-old. It is believed that the learning difficulties that plague some children due to vision or auditory problems might be alleviated with early and proper psychomotor training.

Teaching preschool physical education is more than watching children scamper around a playground and hanging on monkey bars. It involves devising a directed series of psychomotor activities designed to improve coordination of gross and fine muscle movements, to ensure that the socialization process is begun, and to remedy (if possible) those conditions that hamper a child as he or she begins kindergarten. Should you undertake this task, you will need much patience, along with a vast knowledge of a variety of psychomotor activities suitable for different developmental stages.

Elementary School (K-6) Teaching

Elementary schools (usually kindergarten through sixth grade) often employ specialists to teach physical education. These specialists are either physical education majors with a certificate to teach K-6 or elementary education majors with an emphasis in physical education. If you major in elementary education with an emphasis in physical education, you can teach a class (say, fifth grade) or teach physical education. Teaching in the classroom part of the day and teaching physical education for the remainder of the day is quite common.

The usual day of the elementary school physical educator can be described in one word—busy! Classes are about 30 minutes long, with students coming into the gym from their classrooms. Seldom are regular gym clothes worn. The classes are coeducational and vary from 20-35 students. In some schools, students have physical education only two or three times per week, although they will have daily recess. The lessons tend to be active; all students should practice a skill many times, under direct supervision; this is an effective way to learn to perform gymnastic skills, dances, basic movements, and low-organized games. As children reach the higher grades, the emphasis on lead-up games increases, since their physical and social maturity has reached the point of readiness for more highly organized team games. Girls and boys are equally skilled. Students are eager to learn skills and even more eager to participate; the more time you spend in talking, the less time they have to participate! Facilities may not be as spacious as those in junior and senior high schools; the gymnasium often doubles as the cafeteria.

Few elementary schools have a well-organized intramural program; those that do find enthusiastic student response. Administrative problems (lack of money, shortage of facilities, and busing problems) make intramurals difficult. An enthusiastic, dynamic physical educator will see the tremendous value of these activities, however, and usually organizes such a program during the noon hour or before or after school. A recent trend is for elementary physical educators to coach in junior or senior high schools; the great need for coaches necessitates this in some districts.

Special joys and problems are connected with elementary school physical education. By far the greatest joy is the enthusiasm of the students. The problems usually revolve around the lack of facilities and the great number of students you see each week.

Perhaps you remember that when you were in grades K-6 your regular classroom teacher "taught" you physical education. This is still the pattern in many schools, but some evidence shows that students taught by a physical education specialist achieve better results. (If this were not true, it would not speak highly of our specialist, but some studies show no specialist superiority.) Most classroom teachers would prefer not to teach physical education, but until the financial situation eases, there is apt to be only a modest increase in the number of specialists in the near future.

The training of the teacher of elementary physical education is fairly standard throughout the United States. Education courses (featuring characteristics and problems of children ages 5-12) and physical education courses (rhythmic activities, movement education, gymnastics, games of low organization, and lead-up games) are commonly taken. In the better programs, you will be required to work with K-6 children outside of schools, such as in local recreation agencies, the YMCA-YWCA, or Little League. Experiences like these are essential, because they help you determine if you wish to teach and whether you wish to work with this age group. You may have forgotten what K-6 physical education is; for many, trying it is liking it!

Middle School (6-10) or Junior High School (7-9) Teaching

At this level, coeducational programs are offered; virtually no emphasis is placed on movement education skills, although their rapid physical growth and development often cause students to be less well coordinated than they were earlier. The primary activities taught by the physical educator in the six or seven classes per day are team sports and fitness activities. Since this is the age at which team membership is important for social reasons, these activities are stressed. Rhythms, aquatics, gymnastics, and individual activities are important. Extracurricular activities are primarily team oriented, with at least a few athletic teams for both boys and girls sponsored by most schools. Intramural programs have been extremely popular, but the increased number of school teams has reduced this program. Physical educators commonly have coaching as one of their duties. (Not too many years ago, coaching was a part of the job, but the majority of schools now pay for any extracurricular assignments.)

The special joys and problems of the 7-9 or 6-10 program are several. In general, the attitude of the students is decidely in favor of any type of activity. This greatly reduces discipline problems. Most schools have better facilities and equipment than are found in elementary schools, although the size of the classes may be drastically increased. The problems revolve around the physical growth of this age group; the students are so varied in coordination, strength, and social and emotional maturity that it is sometimes difficult to determine what will benefit the most students. Those students who are poor in physical education begin to dislike it, because they are gradually becoming more concerned with peer status than with personal skill attainment. This makes it important for all students to have some degree of success.

This age group, despite its peer-influence problems, lends itself to some individualized programs. Varied activities should be offered. Students need to be exposed to a wide number of activities with the intent that specialization will occur in the next few years as each student develops greater interest in fewer activities. If the program contains only the standard four or five sports, many students will lose interest as they achieve a skill level that satisfies them.

Physical educators at these levels have approximately the same qualifications as do those who teach in the earlier grades: a four-year bachelor's degree. In those states where many out-of-state teachers apply for jobs, often the M.A. or M.S. is necessary.

Senior High School (10-12 or 9-12) Teaching

At the high school level, an emphasis is still on team sports and fitness, but the better programs will feature the individual, dual, and rhythmic areas even more prominently. The carryover sports should receive the primary emphasis, because this is the last time many of the students will take physical education. Many schools combine physical education with health, driver education, and/or first aid. Physical educators or health educators tolerate this arrangement, but many are convinced that these should be separate courses, each taught by a specialist. Intramurals and interscholastic activities are very much a part of the high school teaching position; again, teachers usually receive extra pay for these extra duties.

In most high schools, the joys outnumber the problems in teaching physical education. On the negative side, the most common deterrents to learning are too many students in class and poor and insufficient facilities. Student attitude toward class may be poor, especially if the activities are the same ones that have been taught since elementary school. High school students usually do not like required uniforms; the class details (e.g., calisthenics, tests, drills) often cause discipline problems. Individualized programs, mini-courses (units only three to six sessions long), and contract grading are all techniques employed by successful teachers.

The joys and satisfactions come with being able to work with and to see progress in students—those who are skilled, strong, and coordinated and who can learn many skills, as well as those initially uninterested students who later find success. When the K-12 program shows progression and variety, when it is based on student interests and needs, and when students are expected to meet logical and individualized standards, then many of the problems can be minimized.

Possession of a bachelor's degree is universally required to teach in high school. Schools that are highly desirable (because of location, size, salary schedule, or facilities) can be more selective of the many applications they receive each year; quite often a master's degree plus teaching experience is required for employment. (Ironically, in these days of financial problems, some districts are not hiring teachers with master's degrees. Since the salary schedule indicates that those with a master's degree will earn more money, the school district saves money by hiring those with only bachelor's degrees.)

Teaching at Inner-City Schools

To this point, the material in this chapter has been about the teaching of physical education in the majority of schools in the United States. We believe that it is a realistic and accurate portrayal, although it obviously is a composite picture. The majority of Americans live in the 25-30 larger cities, however—and schools in these cities are sometimes strikingly different from those portrayed here. The students are somewhat different; the schools are different. It stands to reason that the programs, too, are different.

In financially burdened inner-city elementary schools, there are often no physical education specialists. The classroom teacher must conduct physical education either on a small asphalt playground or in a multipurpose room that also serves as a lunchroom and assembly hall. The outdoor facilities (smaller), the bilingual students, the student nonparticipation in class, the students' poor nutrition and inadequate rest, and the lower degree of parental guidance or concern combine to produce active, but unmotivated students. Teaching physical education in inner-city elementary schools is more difficult, more discouraging, and more frustrating than teaching in other situations—but it is probably more essential.

In junior and senior high schools, the student problems are compounded by the condition of the old buildings. "White flight" from the cities has caused minority children to become the majority in inner-city schools. Racial clashes are common, often with tragic results. The problems of the elementary schools are all present, plus greatly increased incidence of pregnancies, use of drugs and alcohol, smoking, and a high dropout rate.

As essential as psychomotor skill development is for all students, human development is even more important to these children. The successful secondary teacher, according to Ridini and Madden (1975), must provide meaningful motivation, a diversified and relevant curriculum, awareness of how physical education activities can carry over into leisure pursuits, and help for those students who cannot perform basic skills at minimal levels. Possessing the attitudes and skills of a counselor is perhaps more important for a successful inner-city physical educator than being a skilled activity teacher. Special techniques are needed, because students will not simply line up in clean uniforms, dutifully go through five minutes of calisthenics, and then move quickly and silently to their squad positions. This is not to say that you would not teach skills or emphasize the cognitive domain. The point is that the affective domain is more crucial; inner-city (especially ghetto) children have so many environmental handicaps that physical education must be more than merely learning the skills and rules of a sport. An excellent source of information on this topic is Ridini and Madden's book (1975), *Physical Education for Inner City Secondary Schools*, which describes the problems and also suggests realistic solutions.

Teaching in Two-Year Colleges

Junior and/or community colleges are springing up all over the United States. These schools almost always offer activity courses for nonmajors and a few courses for majors. Teachers in junior college invariably have a master's degree and often have had experience in the K-12 program. Coaching and/or supervising intramurals is a common assignment for both men and women. The junior colleges usually offer such courses as introductory physical education, first aid, and anatomy and physiology for the prospective major, as well as activity courses for all. Junior college teachers should be motivated toward teacher preparation, as well as toward general teaching. The junior college is often a part of the local district, and its teachers are on the same salary schedule as other teachers in the district.

The primary difference that you would note if teaching in college is the absence of discipline problems. Most teachers find this a refreshing change! The junior college commonly requires all students to take one (sometimes two) years of physical education activity courses. Since these are apt to be single courses (e.g., beginning tennis), the junior college teacher begins to specialize. A shortage of expert teachers in gymnastics, karate, SCUBA, fencing, and rhythms exists, while teachers with expertise in team sports are plentiful.

Teaching in Four-Year Colleges

The physical education department at a four-year institution has two primary missions—to offer service courses to the general student body and to offer courses for physical education majors. Very rarely are teachers without master's degrees hired for the four-year colleges; the doctorate is highly desirable if a person is to be promoted and receive an adequate salary. The small college hires generalists (persons who can teach or coach a variety of different activities), whereas the larger college or university will hire research and teaching methodology specialists as well as experts in such activities as gymnastics, aquatics, individual sport, and dance.

Coaching as an extracurricular duty is most often combined with teaching at the smaller schools. Although athletics has grown into a large business at the major universities, that often means that there is no connection between physical education and athletics. Coaching at all levels will be discussed in detail later in this chapter.

As at other levels, teaching in college has both joys and problems. Discipline problems are minimal, and the facilities and equipment are superior to those at most high schools. The teaching load is somewhat less than in the K-12 grades, ranging from 12 classroom hours per week to about 20. This figure varies greatly, depending upon coaching duties, teaching graduate courses, administrative responsibilities, and institutional policies.

TEACHING OVERSEAS

The U.S. government has need for a number of teachers in overseas positions. The Department of Defense maintains over 275 dependents' schools (kindergarten through community college) in 22 foreign countries, most of which include physical education teachers among their faculty. Because of staffing needs, those who wish to teach high school physical education must be qualified to teach in at least one other area. Teaching duties, salaries, facilities, etc., are comparable to those in the United States.

The Peace Corps has much fewer opportunities for physical educators. Most of these positions are in the emerging nations of Africa and Asia and involve much more than teaching. Coaching, teaching native teachers, raising funds, etc., are all part of the job. Salaries are lower and fringe benefits are less impressive than in other teaching situations.[1]

TEACHING SPECIALISTS

Currently in American society, there is a tremendous increase in opportunities to specialize in teaching one particular sport. You may recall (Chapter 4) that during the 1800s and early 1900s a number of private gymnastic groups were

---

[1]For information about overseas teaching assignments, contact Department of Defense Dependents' Schools, 2461 Eisenhower Ave., Alexandria, VA 22331; or Peace Corps, Washington, DC 20525.

sponsored by certain ethnic groups; by and large, these have been replaced by numerous racquetball clubs, health spas, swim schools, and dance studios. Persons who teach in these sites are specialists in one particular activity.

Specialization has both advantages and disadvantages. Teaching the same activity day after day enables you to become an expert. You will learn numerous techniques for teaching persons of widely differing abilities, have an opportunity to meet the nationally known performers, and, in general, be considered the local leader in this activity. A possible disadvantage relates to the monotony of specializing in only one activity—but, for some, the repetition does not become boring. A specialist normally earns more through exhibitions, private lessons, and clinic appearances than do teachers of physical education. One disadvantage is lack of security, as specialists are generally hired on a month-to-month basis or at most on a one-year contract. Finally, most specialists sell memberships, maintain facilities, or work behind a desk in addition to teaching. This may or may not be desirable, depending on the individual.

Regardless of the pros and cons, many physical education majors wish to spend at least a few years specializing in one particular activity. Table 12.1 lists the career opportunities that are most promising in terms of numbers of available jobs. Remember, however, that there are persons who specialize in virtually every sporting activity known.

THE RESEARCHER AND SCHOLAR

Until recently, universities hired physical education faculty members on the basis of their ability to teach activities rather than on their scholarly and/or creative abilities. Nowadays, however, college faculty members are expected to teach as well as contribute professionally by writing, doing research, and serving in professional groups. Recently hired physical educators have had to conform to this expectation; thus there are a growing number who consider themselves scholars and researchers. They usually possess the doctorate degree in a specialty (e.g., sport psychology or sociology, exercise physiology, psychomotor behavior, administration, curriculum) and devote their energies to securing grants and to investigating various aspects of their interest. Publishing (either articles or books) and speaking to professional groups is expected. These faculty members are not hired only to teach activity courses, although most have expertise in at least one area and actually teach one or two classes during a year.

COACHING

Definitions

The following terms will be used as we discuss athletic coaching in the United States:

1. *Educational athletics*—The concept that the purpose of school athletics is educational in nature. This implies that athletic participation develops desirable physical, social, and emotional characteristics, regardless of

TABLE 12.1. CAREER OPPORTUNITIES FOR SPORT TEACHING SPECIALISTS

TEACHING SPECIALTY	TYPICAL EMPLOYER
Dance	School: large high school, school district Private group: dance studio, dance company, health spa Government: city recreation department Agency: YMCA, YWCA
Fitness and Exercise	
Adult	School: school district, college Private group: health spa, athletic club, exercise center Government: city recreation department Agency: YMCA, YWCA
Senior citizen	School: college Private group: retirement center Government: city recreation department Agency: YMCA, YWCA
Golf	School: college Private group: country club, driving range, golf and tennis club, athletic club Government: public golf course
Gymnastics	Schools: large high school, college Private group: gymnastics school Government: city recreation department Agency: YMCA, YWCA
Handball, Racquetball	School: college Private groups: handball/racquetball club, athletic club Agency: YMCA
Skiing	School: college Private groups: resorts Government: city recreation department
Swimming	School: large junior or senior high school, school districts, college Private group: swim school Government: city recreation department Agency: YMCA, YWCA
Tennis	School: college Private group: tennis club, golf and tennis club, athletic club Government: city recreation department

whether a person or a team wins or loses. Entertaining spectators, making money, or emphasizing athletics over other aspects of the school curriculum is not a part of educational athletics.

2. *Interscholastic or intercollegiate contests*—Games orevents between two or more schools or colleges.

3. *Age-group program*—Organized athletics for participants of certain age groups, most commonly ages 5-12.

4. *Masters' program*—Organized competition for persons 25 years old or older. Track and swimming are the most common competitive programs for adults in the United States.
5. *Coaching certificate*—A certificate earned by a person who has satisfied state education requirements.
6. *Part-time coach*—A person employed by a school or nonschool group only to coach. In most cases, he or she has the qualifications for full-time employment with the group, but for various reasons the coaching is only part-time.

Coaching in Schools

Coaches are found virtually everywhere in American society—from Little League and age-group competitive programs through school and college situations to the professional leagues and to the Masters level. As far as the immediate future is concerned, however, most paid coaching opportunities will be found in school and college situations.

You may be surprised to realize that most nations of the world do not include athletics as part of their school programs. These countries see no relationship between athletics and educational goals, while we believe in educational athletics.

Despite our idealistic view that athletics is educational, there are growing signs that public support is decreasing. This is caused, for the most part, by taxpayer revolt, in which people vote against raising their taxes for school-related purposes. Opponents contend that only a minority of students participate in athletics (this was especially true before Title IX) and/or that athletics has become the "tail that wags the dog," assuming far too much importance in the minds of students.

Annual surveys of participation in high school sports[2] reflect this recent decline in both financial and ideological support. For example, in 1970-1971, 3.7 million boys were on interscholastic teams. By 1977-1978, the number had risen to 4.4 million, but since then, the number has fallen each year, dipping to 3.5 million in 1980-1981.

Participation of girls has followed a similar pattern, except that the decline after 1977-1978 was only temporary. In 1970-1971, 294,000 girls were on high school teams. Primarily because of Title IX, the number rose to 2.1 million by 1977-1978. After a decline for the next two years, the 1980-1981 figure rose to 1.9 million.

Table 12.2 provides a breakdown of participants by sport. As you might expect, the most popular sports are basketball and track and field, plus football for boys and volleyball for girls.

What do these facts and trends mean for you? First, there is now, and will be for some time, a need for coaches at all levels. When you consider that each team has at least one coach and some have several, do you question the need? Second, there has traditionally been a surplus of male basketball, football, baseball,

[2]National Federation of State High School Associations, Kansas City, MO, 1981.

TABLE 12.2. 1981 INTERSCHOLASTIC SPORTS PARTICIPATION SURVEY

	BOYS		GIRLS	
	Number of Schools	*Number of Participants*	*Number of Schools*	*Number of Participants*
Archery	89	220	32	501
Badminton	39	444	554	9,608
Baseball	14,027	422,310		
Basketball	18,041	553,702	16,595	423,568
Bowling	730	6,761	565	6,272
Crew	17	430	4	120
Cross Country	9,952	172,270	6,938	90,224
Curling	3	64		
Decathlon	162	378		
Drill teams			345	9,786
Fencing	47	708	36	504
Field hockey	1	10	1,748	47,688
Football				
11-man	14,169	896,145		
9-man	306	6,738		
8-man	515	12,625		
6-man	61	1,159		
Golf	9,602	118,390	3,048	32,828
Gymnastics	845	13,293	2,990	64,815
Ice hockey	856	25,925	10	56
Judo	13	252	1	3
Lacrosse	416	13,501	177	4,942
Pentathlon			119	266
Riflery	244	2,991	133	795
Rugby	2	42		
Skiing				
Downhill	393	6,487	370	5,136
Cross-country	207	2,575	207	2,434
Soccer	4,555	149,376	1,671	41,111
Softball				
Fast-pitch	26	479	7,293	180,213
Slow-pitch	29	548	1,196	24,218
Swimming and diving	3,726	90,429	3,583	86,853
Table tennis	4	46	2	23
Tennis	9,086	128,417	8,459	118,581
Track and field				
Indoor	1,123	33,275	754	15,464
Outdoor	14,618	507,791	12,365	376,995
Volleyball	671	11,732	11,952	296,291
Water polo	883	26,845	28	243
Weightlifting	177	7,199	21	385
Wrestling	7,900	219,624	1	47

Compiled by the National Federation of State High School Associations, Kansas City, MO. Used by permission.

and track coaches, but a shortage of coaches for female teams in all sports. Professional educators prefer female coaches for female teams. Third, for both sexes there is a shortage of qualified gymnastic, soccer, tennis, and golf coaches.

As mentioned earlier, the majority of males who major in physical education do so with the intent of coaching. More and more female majors now see this as one of their goals. Since virtually all majors have participated in at least one high school athletic team, you undoubtedly are familiar with the duties and responsibilities of coaching.

In bygone days, physical education teachers often coached three sports as a part of their job and in addition conducted the intramural program—all without extra pay. Now coaches and intramural directors are commonly paid in one of two ways: a salary (ranging from as little as $100 to as much as $2,500 for one sport) or a reduced teaching load (a person who coaches will teach one or two fewer classes than other teachers).

Obtaining a coaching job involves a unique problem. Despite the need for more coaches, some superintendents do not hire physical educators as head coaches in the "pressure" sports. The reason is simple: too many of these coaches spend time and energy in coaching, giving second priority to teaching. While employers acknowledge that physical education majors are the best trained coaches, they feel that the attitude of some toward coaching harms the physical education program.

In many high schools of moderate size or smaller, there are but one male and one female physical educator. At the same time, there is a need for head and assistant coaches in many sports. Thus, school districts need coaches, but may not need physical educators. The trend is strong to hire part-time persons certified to coach by having a minor in physical education or a coaching certificate. The coaching certification is a relatively new program; it was created specifically to offer training to those men and women who wish to coach, but who do not necessarily want to teach physical education. In states that have this certification, the law reads that to be a coach in most sports, the person must either be a physical education major, be a physical education minor, or possess the coaching certificate. Because of the overcrowded field in physical education and the great need for coaches, there is an ever-expanding number of coaching-certified people. Regulations vary from state to state, but usually the coaching certificate requires courses in principles of physical education, human anatomy and/or physiology, organization of athletics, athletic training or first aid, and coaching theory courses. If your school offers the coaching certificate, the exact regulations will be given in the college bulletin.

Many persons coach for only a short time. It is a job characterized by personal and public pressure, by the continual striving to win. Granted, winning is an important objective, but often it is detrimental to educational goals. Another reason why coaches change jobs has to do with the changing values of students; more and more students are deciding that the sacrifice, the training, the hard work involved in athletics are not worth the effort. A third reason is the time required to coach successfully. Your desire to spend 20-40 hours per week on athletic matters may decrease as your other responsibilities grow. There may be other reasons, such as inadequate budget, poor facilities, or uneven competition, which results in continual losses. For most coaches, however, these reasons are forgotten because of the satisfactions of associating with student athletes and watching and helping them grow in many ways.

Coaching Overseas

The U.S. government has temporary positions (from three months to two years) for athletic coaches. Many countries, especially the emerging nations, desire American sports knowledge and expertise. The State Department and AAHPERD cooperate in fulfilling these requests, usually by selecting persons who have had successful teaching and coaching experiences. Technical competence is the most important qualification. Common practice is to assign such a person as the national coach of a certain sport; he or she will train and then accompany the teams to national and international sporting events. Should a position such as this hold interest for you, a knowledge of foreign languages will be a great asset. An overseas coach must be resourceful (facilities are poor by American standards), respectful of persons in other lands, and extremely conscientious. In other words, there is no place for an "ugly American" overseas. Salary and other fringe benefits vary tremendously. The number of such positions is quite limited, but for those who qualify, coaching overseas can be a most rewarding experience.[3]

Coaching Professional Teams

Although they receive a great deal of publicity, there are comparatively very few persons who make their living coaching professional athletes. Those who have become head coaches or managers in the major leagues achieve fame and fortune—but they are fired with regularity. Thus, for most persons who aspire to coach, the lack of job security in the professional ranks is a great deterrent. This, along with the excessive time demands of coaching, almost always attracts younger persons who can withstand the rigorous pace with the hope of reaching the top. By far the majority of professional coaches leave the coaching ranks after 5-10 years; for the most part, they enter the business world or sport administration.

PROFILE OF PHYSICAL EDUCATION TEACHERS AND COACHES

Past experience as a student has given you some insight into what you think a physical education teacher and/or coach does, but quite often the view from one perspective is quite different from another. Knowledge of exactly where and what physical educators teach, and of their involvement in duties other than teaching, will serve as a guide as you make decisions about a teaching and/or coaching career. Table 12.3 presents a profile of past physical education teachers and coaches with expectations in 1984.

---

[3]For information about overseas coaching assignments, contact the National Association for Sport and Physical Education (NASPE), AAHPERD, 1900 Association Drive, Reston, VA 22091; or United States Sports Academy, Box 8650, Mobile, AL 36608.

TABLE 12.3. PROFILE OF K–12 PHYSICAL EDUCATION TEACHERS AND COACHES

WHAT WAS TRUE IN 1970–1981	WHAT MIGHT BE TRUE BY 1984
Where do physical educators teach?	By 1984, school age population will decrease (ages 5–13, 11%; ages 14–17, 15%). Enrollment will decrease (K–8, 8%; 9–12, 13%). Teacher need will increase in K–8 by 6%; will decrease by 9% in 9–12 grades.[4]
About 35% teach in K–6 classes, about 50% in 7–10, about 15% in 10–12.[1]	
About 67% of all physical education teachers have taught at each level (elementary, middle school, high school) at some time in their career.[5]	The percentage of physical education teachers at each level will probably remain about the same.
Secondary physical education teachers compose about 8.3% of all secondary teachers.[2]	Many large districts require that teachers (whether new or experienced) begin in the elementary program, and move to the upper grades as positions open.
Elementary physical education specialists who regularly teach physical education are found in 69% of school districts. About 55% of the districts employ specialists who only teach. Elementary specialists who act as consultants and also teach are found in about 5% of school districts. The larger the district, the more likely the consultant or consultant-teacher role is found.[3]	If economic pressures lessen, more elementary specialists will be hired in school districts of every size.
	It will be advantageous for physical education majors who expect to teach in high school to have a second teaching area (minor). Schools need persons to help coach, but will have relatively few full-time physical education openings.
About 74% of all districts have elementary physical education teachers.[3]	Elementary physical education consultants will invariably be those who had had 2–10 years of successful experience.
What do physical educators teach?	Versatility will continue to be a desirable quality.
About 33% teach health and/or first aid.[5]	Great rise in coed, lifetime sports will mean that male and female students in each class will be the norm rather than the exception.
Only about 20% provide an adaptive or corrective program.[1]	
About 50% of the men have, at some time in their careers, taught girls.[1]	There still will be combination physical education-health teachers, but health specialists will be required in many states.
About 25% of the women, have, at some time in their careers, taught boys.[1]	
Team sports are emphasized in grades 7–11.[1] Lifetime sports in grades 10–12.[1]	Recreation responsibilities will be given to recreation specialists, except for summer-only physical activity programs.
	Rise in outdoor recreation (hiking, skiing, mountain climbing) calls for persons to teach these activities.
	Increased need for dance, aquatic (especially SCUBA), gymnastic experts.
	Increased need for those trained to work with the mentally, emotionally, and physically handicapped.
What about coaching athletics, intramurals, cheerleaders?	Great increase in the number of coaching jobs for both men and women. Women especially will probably be required to coach if they want to teach physical education in grades 7–12.
About 55% of the men and women coach one or more varsity sports.[5]	
About 16% of the men coach a girls' varsity sport, and 4% of the women coach a boys' varsity sport.	
About 45% of the men are an assistant coach in at least one sport.[1]	
About 17% of the men are athletic directors.[5]	
About 18% (women) and 24% (men) are also directors of intramural sports.[5]	
About 14% of the women coach cheerleaders.[5]	

TABLE 12.3. (Continued)

WHAT WAS TRUE IN 1970–1981	WHAT MIGHT BE TRUE BY 1984
What do physical educators perceive as their teaching weaknesses? Lack of proficiency to teach adaptive-correctives, dance, rhythms, and elementary physical education.[5] Lack of early (sophomore or junior year in college) professional experiences in school.[5] Lack of experience in successfully coping with other situations than white middle-class suburban students.[1]	Pattern will be to have two athletic directors (one male, one female). Intramural participation will probably decrease as many more school teams are formed. Directing the cheerleaders may still be a required duty for some. Rise of sport and recreation clubs means the need for sponsors, teachers. The rise of opportunity to specialize while an undergraduate will help prepare persons in a chosen activity area. More schools will offer an opportunity to specialize in elementary, secondary, or adaptive physical education. Early field experiences (internships, practicums, prestudent teaching) will be common. Student experiences (student teaching, internships, practica) in inner city, and small rural schools will be "strongly recommended" by the department.

Material for the "What Was True" column was gathered from various sources of 1970–1981 data. Material in the "What Might Be True by 1984" column is an interpretation by a national group and by the authors of this text.

[1]E. Stafford *et al., Educational characteristics of physical education teachers in Wisconsin public schools* (Madison, Wis.: Wisconsin Dept. of Public Instruction, 1970), pp. 8, 9, 13, 18, 21, 31.

[2]*NEA Research Bulletin* (March 1972):4.

[3]*NEA Research Bulletin* (May 1972):45, 46.

[4]National Center for Education Statistics, 1976.

[5]E. Stafford, 1981. Changing trends in Wisconsin physical education *JOPERD* 52 (November-December):29-31.

SALARIES OF PHYSICAL EDUCATION TEACHERS AND COACHES

Salaries have traditionally been low, both for teachers and for coaches. This is partly due to the traditional view that because public employees enjoy job security (e.g., tenure), they should work for less money. Perhaps the lower salaries are explained by the notion that "anybody can teach or coach." In any event, salary is not one of the attractions of either teaching or coaching. Table 12.4 presents a 1982 salary schedule for a moderate-sized school district, along with their pay schedule for extra-duty athletic responsibilities. Use the figures only as guides; remember that local economic conditions influence wages. Read the schedule as follows:

A beginning teacher with no experience would earn $12,500; if the person had 20 credits past the bachelor's degree and had taught for three years, the salary would be $13,770. The maximum salary for a person with a master's degree and no additional credits would be $22,570.

The senior high school activities sheet (Table 12.5) shows the amounts earned by various coaches and coaching assistants. For example, head senior high basketball coaches are paid $1,320-$1,915; golf coaches are paid $720-$1,045; and so on.

TABLE 12.4. TEACHER SALARY SCHEDULES

STEP	B BACH.	C BACH. +20	D BACH. +40	E BACH. +60	F BACH. +80 or MASTER'S	G MASTER'S +20	H MASTER'S +40	I MASTER'S +60	J MASTER'S +80	K EARNED DOCTORATE
1	$12,500	$12,740	$12,980	$13,225	$ 13,410	$ 13,675	$ 13,945	$ 14,280	$ 14,665	$ 14,955
2	13,015	13,265	13,505	13,735	13,960	14,240	14,500	14,970	15,260	15,555
3	13,535	13,770	14,075	14,315	14,520	14,790	15,135	15,560	15,890	16,225
4	14,120	14,340	14,655	14,890	15,155	15,420	15,755	16,235	16,565	16,895
5	14,680	14,930	15,225	15,585	15,770	16,040	16,380	16,900	17,225	17,555
6	15,270	15,500	15,810	16,130	16,405	16,670	17,000	17,570	17,900	18,230
7	15,840	16,080	16,445	16,680	17,020	17,290	17,645	18,235	18,600	18,970
8	16,485	16,720	17,085	17,320	17,715	17,990	18,395	18,975	19,345	19,705
9	17,125	17,365	17,715	17,960	18,410	18,680	19,075	19,710	20,090	20,450
10	17,755	17,995	18,360	18,600	19,095	19,375	19,780	20,455	20,825	21,185
11		18,635	19,005	19,235	19,795	20,065	20,465	21,190	21,565	21,925
12			19,635	19,880	20,495	20,750	21,160	21,945	22,300	22,675
13			20,280	20,575	21,175	21,455	21,985	22,675	23,045	23,415
14			20,920	21,280	21,880	22,145	22,815	23,420	23,785	24,155
15					22,570	22,965	23,635	24,165	24,520	24,890
16						23,795	24,465	24,900	25,340	25,780
17							25,285	25,785	26,295	26,800
									27,245	27,830

Educational lanes are stated in terms of quarter hours.

Source: Poudre R-1 School District, Fort Collins, CO. Used by permission.

JOB SATISFACTION

Job satisfaction among teachers varies greatly with the situation. Parkhouse and Holmen (1980) report that suburban teachers were more satisfied with the intrinsic aspects of their job (work, colleagues, supervision) than they were with their pay. Conversely, inner-city teachers were more satisfied with the pay (which in some cases included extra pay because of the violent nature of some school situations) than they were with their work, colleagues, and supervisors. Although not mentioned by Parkhouse and Holmen, it would appear that teaching specialists are more satisfied with their situations, inasmuch as their students for the most part elect to attend classes (which greatly reduces the discipline problem), and their pay is higher than that of school physical education teachers.

EDUCATIONAL PREPARATION

The theme of this text is that physical education is a discipline and that teachers and coaches should understand all of its aspects. Thus, you should be conversant with the foundations of our area and, in addition, should learn about the special techniques that pertain to teaching and to coaching. Courses in both categories are listed and/or described below.

Human Anatomy, Physiology, Physiology of Exercise. These courses were mentioned in Chapter 6.

TABLE 12.5. EXTRA-DUTY SALARY SCHEDULE

MINIMUM	MAXIMUM	
$ 240	$ 350	Junior high—intramurals
480	700	Boosters; cheerleaders; pep club; junior high assistant in basketball, football, track, wrestling
600	870	Junior high head coach in track, softball, volleyball, wrestling; senior high assistant in cross country, gymnastics, swimming, volleyball
720	1,045	Junior high head coach in basketball, football, track (combined team); senior high head coach in golf, tennis, cross country; senior high assistant in baseball, wrestling
840	1,220	Senior high assistant in track (combined team)
960	1,395	Senior high assistant in basketball, football; senior high head coach in baseball, gymnastics, swimming, track, volleyball
1,080	1,570	Senior high head coach in track (combined team), wrestling
1,200	1,740	Senior high athletic trainer
1,320	1,915	Senior high head coach in basketball, football

Source: Poudre R-1 School District, Fort Collins, CO. Used by permission.

Activity courses in various sports, Psychomotor Learning, Teaching Methods. Although these courses were described in Chapter 7, it is also appropriate to mention methods courses in the context of the present chapter.

Psychology of Coaching. This course (described in Chapter 8) has an obvious relationship to your future.

Physics, Mathematics, Kinesiology. These courses were described in Chapter 9.

Economics, Political Science, Sociology, Sport and Society. These courses were discussed in Chapter 10.

Organization and Administration of Physical Education. Numerous policies and details must be considered when conducting a school physical education program. These pertain to the activity program, the staff, the facilities, intramural and interscholastic athletics, class routines, public relations, and safety precautions.

Measurement and Evaluation in Physical Education. For many, the most difficult problem in teaching is the assigning of grades. Because we can use so many objective devices (stopwatches, tape measures, and the like), it is comparatively easy to measure physical performance. Evaluating and grading it is another matter. In the measurement course, you will learn elementary statistics, the administration and interpretation of all types of skill and written tests, and the principles of testing.

First Aid and/or **Athletic Training.** These courses permit you to deal confidently with the emergencies that are apt to occur.

In addition to the physical education major courses, about one-eighth of the credits required for graduation will be in education. Many students feel that the education courses are too general and irrelevant to physical education and coaching. This is not so. You must know about society and people of all ages to be the best possible teacher and coach.

Coaching Clinics and Activity Workshops

Numerous opportunities exist for out-of-class learning in particular sports. Most clinics and workshops are held on weekends or during vacations and feature prominent coaches or teachers. They are indispensable for learning the latest techniques in a particular sport. Even though most are designed for coaches and teachers who are already employed, students are welcome to attend.

Field Experience

As mentioned earlier, it is essential that you have early experience in schools. We have known students who, after student teaching in their senior year, decided that they did not want to teach. This is a waste of time and money for both the student and the department. Summer recreation experience or coaching Little League is not quite the same as teaching or coaching in a school setting. There is no substitute for actually helping a coach or a teacher, working under their competent supervision.

OTHER TEACHING AREAS

In the past, it was common for physical educators to graduate with a combined health-physical education degree and thus be qualified to teach in either or both areas. This is no longer the case, as most states require a person to have a major to teach in a particular subject area. Because of the science courses (biology, chemistry, physiology) that are required for physical education majors, in some cases teaching in the biological sciences is permitted. Most beginning teaching positions in physical education are not full-time; they are combined with another teaching subject. You will almost always have a second teaching area. This should be chosen on the basis of what is appealing to you and not on the basis of what teaching area appears to have the greatest number of openings. Industrial sciences and business education have been such areas in the past, but conditions constantly change. Select as your second teaching area one that you would like to do full-time--because that is what you may have to do for one or two years, while you wait for the desired physical education and/or coaching position to materialize.

Student Activity

This chapter has outlined various teaching and coaching career opportunities. Select the one that most interests you and submit a written report containing as much of the following material as possible:

1. Observation of the actual situation
2. Interview with someone who is now working (or has worked) in that area
3. Information obtained from the employer or the library
4. Interview with a college student who is preparing for this job.

Statements for Class Discussion

1. Anybody who knows sport skills can teach elementary school physical education.

2. Physical education should be fun, but all we do is practice skills; we never get to play.
3. Physical education is no fun because the athletes get all the attention from the coach.
4. Why should the school hire physical education teachers? All they do is watch kids play games they already know.
5. How do you react to this conversation?
    Person 1: I am a physical educator.
    Person 2: Oh, really? What do you coach?
6. Should a physical educator (who does not coach) be addressed by the students as "Coach"?

Bibliography

GENERAL

AAHPERD. [n.d.] *Physical education careers for women; Careers in physical education and coaching for boys; Dance careers for men and women.* Reston, VA.: AAHPERD. Pamphlets.
———. 1962. *This is physical education.* Reston, Va.: AAHPERD.
Kelley, E. J., and Lindsay, C. A. 1980. A comparison of knowledge obsolescence of graduating seniors and practitioners in the field of physical education. *Research Quarterly for Exercise and Sport* 51 (December): 636-644.
Klesius, S. E. 1971. Physical education in the seventies: Where do you stand? *JOPERD* 42 (February): 46.
National Federation of State High School Associations. 1980. *Sports participation survey.* Cited in National Sporting Goods Association. 1980. *NSGA Memo to Management* 23 (November): 2.
Schochet, M. 1970. We can't remain just a high priced repetitive recreation program. *JOPERD* 41 (April): 24.

AQUATICS

Alexander, R., and Shields, D. 1974. University of Florida aquatic specialist program. *JOPERD* 45 (November-December): 69.
Cahill, P. 1976. Cortland's professional preparation in aquatics. *JOPERD* 47 (May): 58-59.

COACHING
Age-Group

Bula, M. 1971. Competition for children: The real issue. *JOPERD* 42 (September): 40.
Frank, J. 1965. Elementary school—not too early for interscholastic sports. *The Physical Educator* 22 (March): 9-11.
Kaplan, J. 1976. A wintery heritage. *Sports Illustrated* 44 (February 9): 30-36.
Pileggi, S. 1975. Everybody gets to play. *Sports Illustrated* 43 (November 3): 47.
Thomas, J., ed. 1977. *Youth sports guide for coaches and parents.* Reston, Va.: AAHPERD.
Underwood, J. 1975. Taking the fun out of a game. *Sports Illustrated* 43 (November 11): 86-98.

School

AAHPERD. 1970. The coaches and the courts. *JOPERD* 41 (June): 10.
Ashton, S. 1972. The athlete's changing perspective: A student view. *JOPERD* 43 (April): 46.

Barry, J. M. 1975. It's all part of the game. *Sports Illustrated* 43 (October 6): 40-52.

Bucher, C. 1973. After the game is over? *The Physical Educator* 30 (December): 171-175.

Crase, D. 1972. Athletics in trouble. *JOPERD* 43 (April): 39.

Heck, A., et al. 1971. Ethics of competition: Three viewpoints. *JOPERD* 42 (March): 87.

Hoehn, R. 1971. The coach as a psychologist. *Scholastic Coach* 40 (April): 78.

Mudra, D. 1980. A humanist looks at coaching. *JOPERD* 51 (October): 22-25.

Neal, P. 1970. Psychological aspects of coaching women in sports. *JOPERD* 41 (October): 75-81.

Noble, L., and Sigle, G. 1980. Minimum requirements for interscholastic coaches. *JOPERD* 51 (November-December): 32-33.

Porter, C. M. 1972. The coach as character builder. *The Physical Educator* 29 (March): 36.

Rosato, F. 1974. The group process—some suggestions for athletics. *The Physical Educator* 31 (March): 87-89.

Sheehan, T. J., and Alsop, W. L. 1972. Educational sport. *JOPERD* 43 (May): 41.

Stein, B. E. 1972. The cultural crisis in American sports. *JOPERD* 43 (April): 42-44.

Steinmetz, L. L., and Bowen, D. H. 1971. Sports in schools: Jeopardy and uncertainty. *Selling Sporting Goods.* Pamphlet.

Private

Kirschenbaum, J. 1978. They're pooling their talent. *Sports Illustrated* 45 (July 10): 32-38.

McDermott, B. 1975. If your game feels sick, visit Dr. Swing. *Sports Illustrated* 43 (June 2): 61-64.

Wendel, R. 1972. Occupational programs are the future. *JOPERD* 37 (October): 17.

DANCE

Arrow, M. 1981. Teaching dance through sports. *JOPERD* 52 (May): 39-41.

Hayes, E. 1980. Dance educators in higher education. *JOPERD* 51 (October): 59-62.

Marr, M. 1975. Where do they go when the dancing stops? *Dance Magazine* 49 (September): 64-66.

Neal, N. 1978. Men and sports in modern dance. *JOPERD* 49 (January): 72.

Ostlere, R. 1975. Keepers of the flame. *Dance Magazine* 49 (September): 67-70.

Thom, R. 1975. Here today . . . and gone tomorrow. *Dance Magazine* 49 (September): 71-74.

TEACHING
General

Carter, J. A. 1971. Is education preparing teachers for the future, or simply perpetuating the past? *The Physical Educator* 28 (May): 81.

Crase, D. 1971. In search of greatness. *The Physical Educator* 28 (October): 130-132.

Miller, D. 1978. The effective teacher. *The Physical Educator* 35 (October): 147-148.

National Education Association. 1975. Teacher supply and demand in public schools, 1974. *NEA Research Memo* (May): 8.

Parkhouse, B., and Holmen, M. 1980. Differences in job satisfaction among suburban and inner-city high school physical education faculty. *Research Quarterly for Exercise and Sport* 51 (December): 654-662.

Stafford, E., Seefeldt, V., and Jensen, G. 1971. Educational characteristics of physical education teachers in Wisconsin public schools. *JOPERD* 42 (May): 51.

College

Clayton, R. 1980. Professional development, or IRS on the college campus. *Journal of Professional Studies* 5 (February): 1-7.

Elementary School

AAHPERD. 1971. Essentials of a quality elementary school physical education program. *JOPERD* 42 (April): 42.

Trimble, R. T. 1972. Selected research findings with implications for elementary school physical education. *The Physical Educator* 29 (October): 123.

Weber, J. D. 1973. Motivational wizard. *JOPERD* 44 (April): 51-55.

Whitehill, P. 1970. Major in elementary physical education at Eastern Washington State College. *JOPERD* 41 (February): 81-83.

Workman, D. 1968. Comparison of performance of children taught by the physical education specialist and by the classroom teacher. *Research Quarterly for Exercise and Sport* 39 (May): 389-394.

Inner-City Schools

Bell, J. A. 1972. Plato, the ghetto, and physical education. *The Physical Educator* 29 (May): 87.

Ezersky, E., and Thiebert, P. R. 1970. City schools without gyms. *JOPERD* 41 (April): 26.

Ridini, L. 1971. Physical education for the inner city. *The Physical Educator* 28 (December): 176-179.

——— and Madden, J. E. 1975. *Physical education for inner city secondary schools.* New York: Harper and Row.

Wagman, E. 1973. Physical education and the disadvantaged. *JOPERD* 44 (March): 29.

Middle School

Bird, J. 1973. Physical education and the middle school child. *JOPERD* 44 (March): 25.

Stafford, E. 1974. Middle schools: Status of physical education programs. *JOPERD* 45 (February): 25-28.

Preschool

Becker, J., et al. 1974. Childhood education program. *JOPERD* 45 (June): 20-21.

Herkowitz, J. 1970. A perceptual motor training program to improve the gross motor abilities of preschoolers. *JOPERD* 41 (April): 120.

Ward, B. 1975. Implications of physical education for preschool children. *The Physical Educator* 32 (May): 80-83.

Werner, P. H. 1975. Movement experience for preschool children. *The Physical Educator* 32 (December): 182-185.

Secondary Schools

AAHPERD. 1971. Guidelines for secondary school physical education. *JOPERD* 42 (April): 47.

———. 1971. New physical education. *JOPERD* 42 (September): 24.

chapter 13
Health-Related Specialties

INTRODUCTION

Health-related careers have a long tradition in physical education. As recounted in Chapter 4, early leaders in our discipline included medical doctors, who advocated physical education because of its supposed health benefits. The comparatively recent interest in adult fitness activities (see Chapter 6) also developed because of the interest in health. Currently, the terms "wellness" and "holistic medicine" are in common use and indicate the continued concern for fitness. From a career point of view, all of these factors are favorable to you, because physical educators who choose a health-related specialty will be in demand for the foreseeable future.

This chapter will indicate how physical education may be used as the foundation for a number of health-related careers. Concepts for you to understand are given first, followed by a discussion of four major career categories—fitness, sports medicine, rehabilitation, and adapted physical education. Each category mentions specific job titles and the duties, probable employers, job outlook, and educational requirements for each category.

Organizations of interest to those considering a career in a health-related specialty are listed in Appendix B.

CONCEPTS TO BE GAINED FROM THIS CHAPTER

When you have mastered the material in this chapter, you will be able to demonstrate comprehension of these concepts:

1. Because of tradition and the current social climate, health-related careers are logical options for physical educators.

2. At this point, a career in either fitness, sports medicine, rehabilitation, or adapted physical education is or is not an appropriate career goal for you. This is based upon your understanding of the principal duties, probable employers, job outlook, and minimum educational requirements of each category.

FITNESS

Physical education teachers are assumed to be exercise specialists, at least by their students! To the adult public, however, the fitness specialist is someone who, through education and personality, can motivate them to participate in exercises.

The *fitness leader* prescribes exercises for individuals and provides counseling to persons with specific needs. In many instances, such persons also teach sport activities, because exercise is not confined to calisthenics. Traditionally, fitness leaders have been employed by YMCAs, but the recent proliferation of adult programs sponsored by colleges, corporations, hospitals, athletic clubs, health spas, handball/racquetball clubs, park departments, etc., have created many job opportunities. These organizations have discovered that, while it is possible (and cheaper!) for people to exercise on their own, most persons need a support group and a trained leader. It is estimated that there are over 800 health spas and exercise salons in the United States (Henschen 1975). These are well-equipped, clean, and efficiently run gymnasiums and pools, with features (saunas, carpeted floors, chrome equipment, and soft music) designed to attract and keep paying customers. They offer the same type of program (exercise and participation in activities) that could be made available to adults after school hours at many school gyms. Some physical educators consider such commercial establishments undesirable, claiming that the operators are only interested in making money. This charge contains some truth, but if the public is willing to spend money for such purposes, and the school or community government fails to provide the facilities and program, where must the public turn? Trained leadership, both male and female, is needed; physical educators can provide it.

Many corporations have adapted goals such as Xerox's, which is to "improve the physical fitness of our employees so that they may live longer lives, have better performance records and participate more fully in life."[1] One estimate (Malena 1976, p. 2) is that 50,000 U.S. companies spend $2 billion annually on recreation and fitness programs. Some companies purchase memberships for their employees in local YMCA-YWCAs or health spas, while others spend money within the organization. Over 500 companies have full-time fitness and/or recreation directors. These positions are for both men and women, since the company gyms are available to all employees. Some companies have both inside and outside facilities; one insurance company has a running track on the roof of its downtown building! Duties of industrial fitness directors include organizing and supervising exercise programs, teaching sport skills, and motivating employees to begin or to continue activity participation. Some companies have their fitness programs under the supervision of their medical department. This is desirable, because physicians give

---

[1]Mimeographed communication from Xerox Recreation Association, Inc. [n.d.]

stress tests and prescribe fitness programs, while the fitness directors ensure that the advice is followed. Salaries and fringe benefits are, in most cases, superior to those of teachers.

YMCAs that have adult health clubs as part of their services usually have excellent programs, and some Ys also have cardiac rehabilitation programs. Most YMCA physical leaders are specifically trained to conduct safe and effective programs, and they can also assist physicians in fitness testing.

Along the same lines, a few fraternal organizations (e.g., Elks, Eagles) are establishing exercise rooms for the benefit of their members. As yet, no trend is established for trained physical educators to be employed, but as the public becomes more aware of the need for intelligently supervised and organized adult physical fitness programs, opportunities will present themselves.

Salaries and fringe benefits depend solely on the financial condition of the enterprise, but they are generally below those of teachers. Further information and a good discussion of this topic is found in Henschen's article, "Health Spa Certification."

Leslie and McClure (1972) point out that activity needs of citizens extend from preschool through retirement and that physical educators have not recognized the potential careers awaiting them, especially in the older-age setting. The need exists for exercise programs for older citizens who are neither ill nor handicapped; physical educators with training in adult fitness programs, recreation activities, and psychology and motivation will be able to fill this need. Some universities are offering majors in commercial physical education and even certification programs for health spa operators. The courses are combinations of physical education, business management, nutrition, health education, recreation, and psychology.

Competent fitness specialists have at least a bachelor's degree in physical education. They have taken specific courses in anatomy, physiology, aquatics, rhythms, racquet sports, and business. This program does not lead to a teaching degree, even though there are teaching skills involved. Business courses are especially valuable, as exercise programs must be cost effective. Exercise leaders in such places as athletic clubs and YMCAs commonly are involved in many of the business aspects of the operation. An internship, which involves working in a fitness program, is a requirement of all good undergraduate programs.

An *exercise physiologist* is also a fitness specialist, sometimes as an active leader, but more often as the person who supervises and directs the overall fitness programs of colleges, corporations, or clinics. Because of his or her extensive background in physiology and the sciences, the exercise physiologist is qualified to direct the human performance laboratory. This involves supervising assistants who lead the adult fitness and cardiac rehabilitation programs. The laboratory serves as the site for evaluating athletes and others who wish to improve their physical performance, as well as for conducting research. A new responsibility of exercise physiologists is serving as consultants to athletic teams and individuals; this is most desirable because it contributes to the financial support of the laboratory as well as providing the opportunity for research.

Because of the increased competence of exercise physiologists and their acceptance as worthy colleagues by physicians, there will be a slow but steady growth of opportunities for employment in colleges, hospitals, and private clinics. Currently, many persons are preparing for careers in exercise physiology; this will result in an adequate number and perhaps even a surplus of qualified persons.

The educational preparation for a career in exercise physiology includes a strong background in chemistry, human biology, anatomy, and physiology. These courses are all part of a good undergraduate physical education program. Participation in athletics is highly desirable, as it provides the experience base necessary to establish rapport with future clients. The master's and doctor's degrees must be earned, preferably at universities with well-established human performance labs. A strong research background is necessary, as continued professional growth depends on such activity.

SPORTS MEDICINE

Although a fitness specialist may be considered part of a sports medicine team, the term usually refers to the services of a physician or athletic trainer. In the United States, interest in sports medicine is in a stage of rapid growth. Medical clinics devoted to the treatment of sport injuries are now being found in many cities, and professional groups such as the American College of Sports Medicine are attracting many members. The recognition that medicine plays an important role in preventive as well as rehabilitative athletic efforts is shown by the increased status afforded athletic trainers, nutritionists, exercise physiologists, and exercise leaders.

Physicians who specialize in sports medicine devote their medical practice to the diagnosing and treatment of persons who have problems associated with vigorous physical activity. These persons may be children, school or college-age students, professional athletes, or simply adults who are active in athletic endeavors. Sport medicine is an especially attractive specialty to those physicians who are former athletes, because they recognize the need for precise treatment not commonly given by physicians in general practice.

A rapidly growing specialty area is preventive medicine, wherein a physician is interested primarily in maintaining the good health of patients. The tremendous rise in adult physical fitness has encouraged this interest. The preventive medicine specialist may be typified by Kenneth H. Cooper, M.D., who is responsible for the popularity of the aerobics programs, or by William Harris, M.D., a cardiologist, who (along with Bill Bowerman, a physical educator) has popularized jogging in the United States. Although few current physical educators have chosen medicine as a profession, some universities have physicians as members of their physical education departments.

Preventive medicine is a very viable career for persons in our discipline. Some physical educators commonly enter medical schools and eventually specialize in sports medicine or orthopedics. An undergraduate degree, with special emphasis on the sciences, is the basic requirement for medical school. Following an internship and admittance to the practice of general medicine, a specialty in sports medicine may be taken. Besides this formal training, service as a team physician invariably occurs.

The *athletic trainer* is a person qualified by training and experience to supervise the preventive and rehabilitative aspects of athletes. He or she acts as a liaison between coach, physician, and player, seeing that the coach's routine procedures (taping, etc.) are carried out and that the physician's orders are followed. The goal of an athletic trainer is simple—to prevent injuries or to treat and supervise the rehabilitation of injured persons so that they can participate in athletics without further damage to themselves.

The future demand for athletic trainers appears to be good for both men and women. There are so many teams sponsored by most schools that at least one qualified trainer is required. This will prove a great benefit both to coaches and to players. The extra money received for serving as a school athletic trainer is comparable to that of a coach.

What courses are taken by athletic trainers? Aside from the sciences, anatomy, physiology, chemistry and/or physics, courses are required in first aid, athletic training, medical aspects of athletic training, nutrition, and kinesiology. In addition, all recognized programs require several hundred hours of practical experience in the training room.

Some athletic trainers (especially those who work in colleges and with professional teams) are registered physical therapists. Physical therapists have a graduate degree in physical therapy and are qualified to administer all types of rehabilitative procedures. Their training is thorough, primarily because of the rigorous standards required to earn the certificate.

Most athletic trainers, though not physical therapists, have taken physical therapy courses as a supplement to their regular undergraduate degree. Excellent training may be secured at one of the colleges and universities in the United States where the basic requirements of the Certified Athletic Trainer award may be met. These schools conform to the standards of the National Athletic Trainers Association. After graduation, students must pass the national certification examination. Possession of this certificate is a distinct advantage when seeking a job.

THERAPY

Therapy includes five different specialties. Certification programs are available and/or required in all specialties; this ensures that therapists have met certain minimum standards established by their professional group.

A *corrective therapist* assists individuals in overcoming physical or mental disabilities. A corrective therapist uses medically oriented physical education techniques to accomplish this. Corrective therapists have become increasingly involved in adapted physical education and perceptual-motor programs for children. All treatment is given under the direction of physicians.

The basic education requirement is a bachelor's degree from an accredited school with a physical education major. Certification may be earned after completing 400 hours of approved clinical training under the supervision of qualified therapists. Although certification is highly desirable, it is not required for all jobs. As an undergraduate, you will meet the usual requirements for the physical education degree, plus take additional courses in psychology, health, corrective and adapted physical education, and programming for the physically and mentally handicapped. Graduate and advanced degrees are offered by some colleges and universities.

Jobs may be found in hospitals and clinics, governmental agencies, rehabilitation centers, camps, colleges and universities, and public and private schools. Salaries and fringe benefits are comparable to those of teachers. A need at the present time is for corrective therapists, especially in hospitals and rehabilitation centers.

Physical therapists work with patients who have been disabled by illness or accident or at birth. The physical therapist evaluates patients with regard to respiratory, cardiovascular, neuromuscular, neuroskeletal, and sensorimotor functions; on the basis of this evaluation, the therapist and a supervising physician select the appropriate treatments.

Treatment given by physical therapists includes exercises for strength, agility, coordination, motion, and endurance; activities for motor learning; instruction in daily living and use of assistive devices; and application of agents such as heat and cold, sound, and water for pain. An important part of a therapist's job is motivating patients, their families, and those who might help during the treatment period.

There are three levels of physical therapy practitioners: (1) professionally qualified physical therapists, (2) physical therapy assistants, and (3) aides. All programs leading to professional certification require coursework in the basic health sciences and clinical sciences, as well as supervised administration of evaluative and therapeutic procedures. The three common patterns of education are: (1) completion of a bachelor's degree program (four years) in physical therapy, (2) completion of a bachelor's degree in physical education or corrective or occupational therapy, followed by a 12- to 16-month physical therapy program, or (3) completion of a bachelor's degree in a related field followed by a two-year master's degree in physical therapy. Regardless of the route chosen, entering professional physical therapy schools is difficult because of the great number of applicants. A high GPA is essential, and additional practical experience in a related field (e.g., athletic training) is highly desirable. Licensing is required in all 50 states; 49 states require an examination before the license is awarded.

Physical therapist assistant training programs are found in junior and community colleges. A graduate earns an associate degree in physical therapy via a special two-year college program. These persons are skilled technical health workers who assist a physical therapist in treatment and in providing other therapy services.

Physical therapist aides are not licensed, but have completed training in a hospital or clinic. Their primary responsibility is to handle routine tasks and activities that a professional physical therapist has determined, assigned, and supervised.

Opportunities for the employment of physical therapists are found in hospitals, clinics, nursing homes, rehabilitation centers, the armed forces, private and public schools, homes for the aged, and day-care centers. Many of the best athletic trainers in college or professional athletics are physical therapists; their special background makes them essential partners on a sports-injury medical team.

The demand for physical therapists is greater than the supply and will be so for some time to come. Salaries and fringe benefits are equal to those of teaching.

Dance therapists use dance (rhythmic movement) as a psychotherapeutic aid to physical and emotional expression. Communicating through dance has been helpful in alleviating some social, emotional, and physical problems.

A bachelor's degree is a prerequisite for advanced professional study in dance therapy. Undergraduate courses include psychology, anatomy, individual body mechanics, and group dynamics, as well as extensive movement training. These latter courses emphasize a variety of dance forms, techniques, and theories of dance, as well as choreography and improvisation. Modern, folk, and ethnic dancing are invaluable parts of the training for a dance therapist. Introductory dance courses and field trips will be a part of the educational experience. At the present time, there are less than a dozen undergraduate programs in the United States. On the graduate level, you will take courses in theory, practice, and methods of dance, along with research emphasis on human behavior. The graduate experience includes an internship, under supervision, in a clinical setting.

Persons with interest and education in dance therapy will find places of employment among rehabilitation centers, geriatric facilities, psychiatric centers and hospitals, correctional facilities, and mental retardation and developmental centers.

The demand for dance therapists will slowly grow as more medical and psychiatric professionals discover their effectiveness. Salaries and fringe benefits are comparable to those of teachers.

Therapeutic recreationists attempt to bring about behavior changes and promote individual growth and development in special groups of people such as the emotionally and physically handicapped, the disadvantaged, and the elderly. They organize and direct activities (sports, drama, nature, games, arts and crafts) adapted to specific needs. They also work with both community agencies and governmental groups to expand services and facilities for the ill, impaired, handicapped, and disabled.

There is a well-defined, six-step career procedure in therapeutic recreation. The first three levels do not require a bachelor's degree. A therapeutic recreation leader or a therapeutic recreation specialist leader holds the bachelor's degree, while the master therapeutic specialist has had graduate preparation and a minimum of three years of work experience.

In the past, most career opportunities in therapeutic recreation were in the institutional setting. Similar positions and responsibilities in recreation administration and leadership were offered in activity therapy complexes to "captive audiences." The trend today is in the direction of municipal responsibility for special groups. Specialized programs for the handicapped are offered by many public and voluntary agencies as a part of the broad aim to meet the leisure requirements of the total community.

A *cardiac rehabilitation specialist* is a therapist who closely supervises the physical reconditioning efforts of persons who have survived a heart attack or who suffer from other heart problems. Heart patients begin rehabilitation in the hospital, but then receive outpatient treatment in a cardiac rehabilitation center, YMCA, or human performance lab. The specialist carefully follows the directions of the physician, ensuring that energy-expenditure levels are well within safe limits.

Constant attention is paid to safety, as the consequence of inept leadership may be fatal. After months of supervised rehabilitation, it is common for persons to be in better physical condition than they were before their heart problem.

A cardiac rehabilitation specialist was quite often an undergraduate physical education major, a nurse, or other health professional. Graduate-level training then provides a thorough background in emergency treatment of heart patients, exercise physiology, stress testing, and exercise prescription writing. Several U.S. colleges and universities offer graduate degrees in this specialization, with the American College of Sports Medicine serving as the certifying agency. Summer programs are offered at various sites throughout the nation, so that persons may receive the training without resigning from their regular positions.

Career prospects for cardiac rehabilitation specialists are bright, because, as the adult population increases in number each year, the incidence of heart problems will also rise. The past few years have actually seen a decrease in the number of deaths due to heart attacks; this was caused in part by better initial fitness levels of adults and better rehabilitation programs conducted by specialists.

ADAPTED PHYSICAL EDUCATION

Teaching physical education to handicapped persons is the specialty of the *adapted physical educator*. This may be a part-time position (combined with teaching those who are not handicapped), but most often it is a full-time position requiring travel to various sites where such persons attend school or classes.

> Adapted physical education consists of a diversified program of developmental activities, games, sports, and rhythms suited to interests, capacities, and limitations of students with impairments, disabilities, or handicaps who may not safely, successfully, or with personal satisfaction engage in unrestricted activities included in general physical education programs (AAHPERD 1975, p. 5).

Obviously the scope of this program is very broad because it serves such a variety of students. Its necessity is readily apparent when one realizes that adapted physical education is needed by 20 to 25 percent of all students. It deals with persons with vision, hearing, and social problems in an attempt to show them educational skills (Winnick 1972, p. 46).

The goal of such a program is to adapt a physical education program to the needs and abilities of the students. These adaptations are of many types: emphasis on basic coordination, revising rules of regular games, physical fitness activities, and rehabilitation exercises. Because of the interest initiated by the Kennedy Foundation—President Kennedy, you may remember, had a sister who is mentally retarded—there has been an upsurge of interest in this specific area.

For those who plan to work in adapted physical education programs, job opportunities are many. Schools must meet stricter governmental regulations that require *all* students to be educated, sometimes within the regular class (mainstreaming). In larger schools, special classes are taught by specialists. These people have the regular physical education major background, supplemented by course-work in psychology of exceptional children, learning disabilities, percep-tual-motor development, remedial exercises, etc. Practical work while an undergraduate is a necessity. Many physical education departments and local school districts sponsor programs specifically for the handicapped. The opportu-nities for such practical experience are numerous; after participating in them you will have a good idea if teaching adapted physical education is an appropriate career for you.

Specialists working in schools receive the same pay and benefits as the regular staff with similar education and service; specialists are expected to meet the same standard of education. Only the larger districts are likely to hire full-time adapted physical education specialists.

Student Activity

This chapter outlines several career possibilities. Select the one that interests you the most and submit a written report containing as much of the following material as possible:

1. Observation of the actual situation
2. Interview with someone who is now working (or has worked) in that area
3. Written information obtained from the employer or library
4. Interview with college students who are preparing for this job.

Statements for Class Discussion

1. If you know how to do exercises, you can lead them so that youth and adults will enjoy them.
2. An exercise physiologist is more valuable to an athletic team than an athletic trainer (or an athletic trainer is more valuable) because _____.
3. A therapist (dance, recreation, physical, corrective, cardiac rehabilitation) is basically a teacher who works with the handicapped.
4. Every physical education teacher should also be an adapted physical education specialist.

Bibliography

FITNESS

Backes, C. 1978. The science of athletics. *TWA Ambassador* (January): 37-39.
Cook, R., et al. 1979. Employee health and fitness program at the Sentry Corporation. *Health Education* (July-August): 4-5.
Henschen, K. 1976. Health spa certification. Pp. 47-55 in Dougherty, N., ed. *Careers in physical education.* Rutgers, N.Y.: NCPEAM.
Leslie, D. K., and McClure, J. W. 1972. The preparation of physical educators for expanded leadership and service roles. *JOPERD* 43 (November-December): 71-72.
McDermott, B. 1980. If you plan to run far and fast, put stress on the testing of your body first. *Sports Illustrated* 47 (June 6): 4.
Malena, D. (ed.). 1976. Just how fit are you? *Datsun Action* 2: 2-3.

Moore, K. 1974. A run for their money. *Sports Illustrated* 41 (November 4): 68-78.

Noland, M. 1978. What physical educators should be teaching about health clubs and figure salons. *JOPERD* 49 (May): 82-86.

Ryan, A. 1980. Employee fitness programs. *The Physician and Sportsmedicine* 8 (May): 64-72.

Van Noy, G. 1981. Getting tested: A personal measure of fitness. *Swim Swim* 3 (Winter): 13-15.

SPORTS MEDICINE AND ATHLETIC TRAINING

Barry, J. M. 1975. It's all a part of the game. *Sports Illustrated* 42 (October 6): 40-42.

Clancy, W. G. 1980. Total sports medicine programs today involve a multi-faceted approach. *Athletic Purchasing and Facilities* 8 (March): 10-12.

Kegerreis, S. 1981. Sports medicine: A functional definition. *JOPERD* 52 (May): 22-23.

Koenigsberg, R., and Arrighi, M. 1975. Women athletic trainers. *JOPERD* 46 (January): 51-52.

Kram, M. 1976. The face of pain. *Sports Illustrated* 43 (March 18): 60-66.

Rumph, R. 1974. The training room staff. *JOPERD* 45 (October): 30-31.

Shaffer, T. E. 1979. The physician and sports medicine. Chap. 1 in *Sports medicine for children and youth*. Columbus, Ohio: Ross Laboratories.

Spiker, J. C. 1979. Athletic trainer education. *JOPERD* 50 (September): 72.

REHABILITATION
Dance Therapy

AAHPERD. 1975. *Careers in activity and therapy fields.* Pamphlet. Reston, Va.: AAHPERD.

Anon. 1976. What is dance therapy? *JOPERD* 47 (January): 39.

Archombeau, M. K., and Szymanski, D. 1977. Dance therapy and the autistic child. *JOPERD* 48 (September): 54-55.

Leventhal, M. 1980. Dance therapy as treatment of choice for the emotionally disturbed and learning disabled child. *JOPERD* 51 (September): 54-55.

Schmais, C. 1973. Dance training for the dance therapist. *JOPERD* 44 (October): 67-68.

————. 1977. Dance therapy as a career. *JOPERD* 48 (May): 38.

Thom, R. A. 1975. Dance therapy. *Dance Magazine* 49 (December): 77.

Physical Therapy

Krumhausl, B. R. 1978. *Opportunities in physical therapy.* Skokie, Ill.: National Textbook Co.

Schleichkorn, J. 1979. What you should know about physical therapy. *JOPERD* 50 (January): 73.

Therapeutic Recreation

Harsanyi, S. 1979. Practice and promise of therapeutic recreation. *JOPERD* 50 (April): 19-23.

ADAPTED PHYSICAL EDUCATION

Austin, D. 1978. A developmental physical education program. *JOPERD* 49 (February): 36-37.

Freischlag, J. 1974. Competition and physical education for the handicapped: How compatible are they? *The Physical Educator* 31 (March): 42-43.

Stein, J. 1976. Sense and nonsense about mainstreaming. *JOPERD* 47 (January): 43.

Winnick, J. 1972. Issues and trends in training adapted physical education personnel. *JOPERD* 43 (October): 75.

chapter 14
Sales and Management

INTRODUCTION

Throughout the United States, a career in sales and/or management is the goal of many. Because of the tremendous public interest and participation in sport and physical activity, careers in either category are quite appropriate for physical educators.

Sport salespersons may be individuals who sell directly to the customer, as in a sporting goods store, or they may travel to various cities calling upon buyers or officers of athletic teams. Quite often, salespersons become owners/managers of a store or company; they then become responsible for the total operation of the business, rather than primarily for selling merchandise.

Regardless of their precise job, sport salespersons deal in a variety of merchandise and services. They are in contact with all segments of the public, from youth sport programs through adult bowling leagues, from hikers and campers to marathon runners to boating enthusiasts. Surely every family in the United States has some type of sports equipment that was bought with the assistance of a sport salesperson.

A sport manager has such a variety of duties that they touch on at least three career categories—communication, sales, and management. Sport administrators must be communication-minded, which means either performing (or supervising others) in the promotion of the program or informing the public about those programs. Sales is an obvious component of most administrator's jobs because customers (whether as spectators or as participants) must be attracted. Most important of these duties is the management aspect—the responsibility for decisions about personnel, finances, and facility that affect the financial success of the enterprise.

This chapter will begin with a listing of concepts to be understood, followed by discussions of the duties, employment conditions, and educational requirements of jobs found in the sales and management career categories.

Organizations and professional groups of interest to sales and management persons are listed in Appendix C.

CONCEPTS TO BE GAINED FROM THIS CHAPTER

When you have mastered the material in this chapter, you will be able to demonstrate comprehension of these concepts:

1. Careers in sales and/or management represent logical choices for those persons interested in applying business skills to sport and physical activity.
2. At this point, a career in either sales or management does or does not interest you, based upon your tentative understanding of the duties, employment conditions, and educational preparation required.

SALES

Contrary to the "Music Man" stereotype, *salespersons* are not unscrupulous swindlers whose only concern is to make a sale and then disappear. The great majority are professionals—that is, they are knowledgeable about their products or service, they have the ability to convince the buyer that the asking price is fair, and they will make every effort to satisfy the customer.

Salespersons sell various types of sporting goods (e.g., racquets, SCUBA gear, camping supplies) to the general public, and in some cases they prepare bids (which are agreements to sell a quantity of goods) for team and group orders. In most cities, there are smaller sporting goods stores where the owner remains active in selling, as well as serving as the buyer, advertising manager, etc.

Even though business is one of the basic areas of our economy, employment of salespersons rises and falls according to economic factors like other types of employment. At the very least, there should be increases in the number of sport sales positions each year, because annual sales in virtually all categories of sporting and recreational goods are showing moderate increases. There is every reason to believe that this trend will continue. Employment is often part-time for beginners, especially during promotional or vacation periods, but experienced salespeople work full-time the year round.

A "sales personality" (the ability to interact with customers and to convince them that the product is suitable for their needs) is the basic qualification for becoming a successful salesperson. Because knowledge of the product is obviously of importance, it is usually better to begin a sales career as a generalist and then become a specialist. Thus, a broad background in many physical activities and sports is most desirable. In what activities should you participate? The answer is obvious— those enjoyed by millions of Americans, because sooner or later they will be in the market for equipment and/or services. Participation changes each month, but one typical summer month (July 1980) found between 2 million and 110 million Americans participating in *each* of these activities: archery, baseball, softball, bowling, camping, darts, general exercise, fishing, football, golf, hunting, jogging/running, racquetball, roller skating, soccer, swimming, table tennis, tennis, and volleyball (*The Sporting Goods Dealer*, October 1980, p. 77). Other months see ice hockey, ice skating, skiing, boating, dancing, handball, and gymnastics added to the list. Participation on your part, including tournament experience, will someday prove beneficial in making a sale.

In most cases, beginning salespeople are paid an hourly wage. As they gain experience, it is common for salespeople to be paid a commission (percentage of the sales) plus a salary, or sometimes a commission only. Most good salespersons will earn more on a commission basis than they will on a salary. For example, a 1980 Dartnell Corporation survey found that salespersons who were paid a salary only averaged $22,000; those on salary plus commission averaged $28,500, and those only on commission averaged $32,000. These salaries pertain to both in-store and traveling salespersons; those who sell only in a retail store will earn about one-half of the amounts mentioned.

A sports department supervisor is sometimes employed by a larger store. He or she is responsible for the sales of a specific department (e.g., hunting equipment, swimwear, golf supplies). Supervisors are in charge of training new salespeople, ordering and shelving merchandise, dealing with customer complaints, and selling merchandise. Qualifications include·experience as a salesperson plus a good business sense, developed through education and training. The ability to direct and to motivate employees is essential, because all sections in the store are evaluated on profitability, which in turn depends upon the efforts of the employees. Some department supervisors receive a monthly salary plus a yearly bonus, others are on salary alone. In either case, they receive about 50 percent above the amount paid to salespeople.

A *sales representative* is a person who calls on buyers for stores, recreation departments, athletic directors, coaches, or owners of sport facilities. Samples of merchandise are displayed, orders taken, and sometimes deliveries are made at a later date. Because the sales "rep" is the only link between the buyer and the manufacturer, he or she must demonstrate new products, make suggestions on advertising and displays, handle complaints about defective merchandise, etc.

Traveling sales reps are employed full-time by manufacturers, by large full-line sporting goods stores, or by sales groups (companies composed of one or more reps who sell the products of several manufacturers). They must have knowledge of the products made or sold by the company, plus the ability to sell. Since constant traveling is difficult work, a certain amount of physical vigor is required.

Reps are almost always paid on commission, in addition to receiving an expense account. Their earnings are high, as indicated by the survey mentioned in the previous section.

An *owner/manager* oversees all aspects of the operation (personnel, advertising, sales, expenses, inventory, control, facility upkeep, etc.). A background in sales and business management and familiarity with the products are essential for success, along with the ability to select good employees. Most owners/managers put in long hours, as their responsibility requires constant alertness to all events in the store. In return for this heavy responsibility, owner/managers enjoy above-average financial returns. Often, they will receive a monthly salary plus a year-end bonus, based upon the profitability of the enterprise.

Desirable educational preparation for salespersons, sales reps, and owner/managers will include a college degree combining business administration and physical education. Courses should be taken in accounting, personnel management, business law, financial management, advertising, and marketing. In physical education, a wide variety of activities should be taken, along with courses in organization and administration of athletics, sport sociology, and facilities construction and management.

Because opportunities for salespersons are found in every city and town in the United States, there are no geographic barriers to employment, but there are obvious limitations. Ski stores are not common in Alabama, and yachting salespersons are rare in Montana! Traveling reps are also found throughout the United States, but are usually centrally located in their geographic area. For example, sales reps in Iowa would probably live in or near Des Moines, while Pittsburgh would be the home of those who travel the western part of Pennsylvania.

As in other careers, there are natural progressions as experience warrants. Most salespeople begin by working part-time in stores that sell various types of merchandise. They eventually become assigned to the sporting goods section of the store or change employers so that they can work exclusively in sporting goods. Part-time sales experience leads to full-time work, which in turn can lead to a choice—remaining in the store or becoming a traveling representative. After experience is obtained, a supervisory position in a store is often attained. In some cases, reps tire of the constant travel and choose an in-store job. Becoming a buyer for the store, then sales manager, and finally store manager are the logical and desirable steps that should be taken before becoming a store owner.

MANAGEMENT

A *sport manager* (or *sport administrator*) is a person who assumes responsibility for part or all of the organizational and administrative details of a sport group or facility. For example, the owner(s) of an athletic club will employ some or all of these persons—a manager, a business manager, a facilities manager. Each of these persons is a sport administrator, responsible for a particular aspect of the operation.

Only a very few sport managers are known to the general public, prominent examples being Pete Rozelle of the NFL or George Steinbrenner of the New York Yankees. Yet, there are hundreds of such persons employed by school districts, colleges and universities, YMCAs, and private physical activity centers (e.g., tennis clubs, swim schools, dance studios). In addition, there are positions with numerous major and minor league professional teams in football, baseball, soccer, basketball, and ice hockey. Sport administrators are not the athletes, coaches, or teachers employed by these groups; they are persons employed behind the scenes who make certain that the sport groups continue to operate—hopefully, at a profit!

The *chief administrator* of a sport group can have such titles as *owner, general manager, athletic director, intramural director, executive director*. The duties are the same, however—to assume overall responsibility for the entire program, focusing special attention on financial and personnel matters. The chief administrator must see that the objectives of the program are met and that the operation is on a sound financial basis. A great deal of public relations work is involved. Most chief administrators spend 50-75 hours per week promoting and overseeing the many facets of the operation.

Although business experience is more important than knowledge of the sport, successful sport administrators have both. Along with these two qualifications, the more ability and experience a person has in promotion and public relations, the better.

An often overlooked essential qualification for those who own or manage private sport centers or professional teams relates to financial resources. Building a tennis or swim center could easily cost $250,000; a health club, even more. These amounts do not include operating funds. Thus, it is apparent that the chief administrator must be able to manage large sums of money successfully, and in some cases to raise the money for operating expenses.

In the past, *school athletic directors* were ex-coaches or former players who knew much about competing in athletics but little about business. This is less true today, as athletic programs must be financially strong and operated at least at a "break-even" point.

Earnings for sport administrators are moderate to high, depending on the group's financial condition. Many chief administrators in professional sports or private activity centers are paid on a "salary plus bonus" arrangement, in which year-end profits determine the size of the bonus.

Special mention must be made of *school intramural directors* or *corporation recreation directors*. Such programs have as their goal 100 percent participation of the group, which means that a wide variety of activities must be offered. Because the directors of these programs are usually hampered by lack of funds, facilities, and personnel, they must be especially resourceful. In many school situations, intramural participation is decreasing, as students prefer to play on school teams. The greater number of school teams also reduces the time available for use of the facilities by other groups. On the other hand, the number of recreation programs sponsored by companies continues to rise, as these programs constitute a very desirable fringe benefit for workers.

Educational preparation is concentrated on business and communication, as well as the particular physical activity sponsored by the group. Because of the greater financial and personnel responsibilities, it is essential that continued growth in business expertise is maintained. Special courses, conferences, workshops, etc., all contribute to a person's ability to keep up with the pressures and demands of modern sport administration.

Administration of sport business affairs is a category involving at least three different job titles. The *business manager* and the *ticket manager* (sometimes the same person in small organizations) are responsible for distinct aspects of the operation. The business manager oversees all financial matters, with the other two persons being subordinate. Operating expenses, salaries, insurance, budgeting, taxes, inventory, and income from tickets and promotions are only some of the items that must be carefully monitored by one or more of these persons. Obviously, a strong business background is essential. College courses in all aspects of finance (e.g., insurance, investments, accounting) provide the basic education.

A *facility director* works for the group that owns the sport center. Sometimes this is a college or a specific corporation; at other times it is a city facility that may be rented to groups for particular events. In either case, administrative duties are numerous, involving preparation of the site before a contest, clean-up, and continual maintenance. Educational preparation involves courses in sanitation, horticulture (for outdoor facilities), mechanics, and maintenance.

Salaries for business managers, ticket managers, and facility directors are minimal, unless the organization is large.

While sport activities are found in virtually every city and town in the United States, most management opportunities are found in the larger (over 50,000) population centers. Consolidated high schools often have a person designated as an athletic director, although this job is usually combined with teaching and/or coaching. Obviously, the larger population centers will have the greater number of schools, recreation departments, and the most private sport facilities (tennis centers, swim and golf clubs). Each of these organizations needs several different sport administrators. There are truly no geographic limitations for employment—every locale has a school or an adult sport program and has need for one or more administrators.

Almost all sport administrators were or are participants in one or more sport activities. Their skill level (whether beginner or professional) is really unimportant, however; for example, very few professional football or baseball players have risen to the rank of general manager of a team. Sport administrators begin by participating in athletics, by becoming involved in the details of the contest (keeping statistics, being an equipment manager), or by serving behind the desk or teaching in a YMCA. After high school and college experience in the intramural and/or athletic program, most administrators become paid members of an athletic system, serving as sport information directors, sports editors, facility managers, activity directors, or instructors. Eventually, many rise to the top of their group, becoming the chief administrator.

An alternate career route is to enter a sport group from the business field, perhaps having little previous involvement with the activity. In these cases, prior success as a business or professional person (e.g., top insurance seller, general manager of a corporation, attorney) is attractive to the owner. He or she knows that business ability is more important than knowledge of the sport.

Student Activity

This chapter has outlined different jobs in the sales and management categories. Select the one that interests you the most and submit a written report containing as much of the following material as possible:

1. Observation of the actual situation
2. Interview with someone who is currently working or who has worked in that area
3. Written information obtained from the employer or library
4. Interview with a college student who is preparing for this career category.

Statements for Class Discussion

1. I would (would not) like to sell sporting goods because _____.
2. Salespersons in sporting goods stores don't know any more about the equipment they sell than I do.
3. An athletic director without coaching experience is like a fish out of water.
4. The owner/manager of a racquetball club should be a certified physical education teacher.

Bibliography

SALES

Anon. 1980. Future trends in courtwear. *Racquetball Industry* 3 (September-October): 10-15.
Epstein, C. 1980. Gymnastics: Sport in transition. *Selling Sporting Goods*[1] 33 (November): 28-30.
Goldman, G. 1981. No sales final: Take it back. *The Sporting Goods Dealer* 163 (February): 37-39.
Gorsuch, L. A. 1981. Employee training: Who's minding the store? *The Sporting Goods Dealer* 164 (May): 41-44.
Quinton, J. 1979. *Retail advertising: The how and why.* Chicago: National Sporting Goods Assn.
———. 1981. Nine common advertising mistakes. *Sports Retailer* 34 (February): 41-43.
Reed, J. D. 1974. How about a game? *Sports Illustrated* 41 (December 12): 78-85.
Schultz, A. 1981. Racquetball pro shops. *Sports Retailer* 34 (May): 47-49.
Spomer, J. 1975. *Athletic clothing facts. Athletic equipment facts. Athletic footwear facts.* Chicago: National Sporting Goods Assn.

MANAGEMENT

AAHPERD. 1970. Professional preparation of the administrator of athletics. *JOPERD* 41 (September): 20.
Deford, F. 1975. No death for a salesman. *Sports Illustrated* 43 (July 28): 56-65.
Kelly, T. B. 1975. Athletics: Leadership or management. *JOPERD* 46 (April): 21.
Kraft, G., and Mason, J. 1981. An activity center that generates revenue. *JOPERD* 52 (May): 11-14.
Richardson, D. E. 1971. Preparation for a career in public school athletic administration. *JOPERD* 42 (February): 17.
Sisley, B. 1975. Challenges facing the woman athletic director. *The Physical Educator* 32 (October): 121-123.
Yates, B. 1973. Shall we gather at the squash courts? *Sports Illustrated* 38 (May 7): 90.

INTRAMURALS AND SPORT CLUBS

Cooney, L. 1979. Sports clubs: Their place within the total intramural-recreational sports program. *JOPERD* 50 (March): 40-41.
Maas, G. 1980. High school intramurals—an endangered species. *JOPERD* 51 (March): 52-53.
Shields, E. 1979. Intramurals: An avenue for developing leisure values. *JOPERD* 50 (April): 75-77.

[1]This publication is now called *Sports Retailer.*

PROFESSIONAL PREPARATION

Anon. 1978. Professional preparation in athletic administration and sport management. *JOPERD* 49 (May): 22-27. An article with the same title, listing Canadian professional preparation programs, appeared in 1979 in *JOPERD* 50 (March): 22-23.

————. 1980. Studying sports administration. *Athletic Purchasing and Facilities* 4 (March): 54-60.

chapter 15

Performing and Sports Communication

INTRODUCTION

The dream of many an athlete is to be a famous professional performer—the star of the ice show, the high-scoring basketball player, the golfer on TV. Few achieve such a lofty goal, but for those who do, a background in physical education and business is most appropriate. A more realistic goal, in terms of employment opportunities, is that of a sports communication specialist—a TV or radio sportscaster, a writer, a sports information director. These people are able to combine their sport skills and their technical competence in communication skills into a viable career.

This chapter will discuss careers in both the performing and the sports communication categories. Concepts will be presented first, followed by a listing of duties, probable future opportunities, and desirable educational preparation.

Most professional athletes and sports communication persons do not major in physical education while in college. We would recommend that college courses in physical education be taken, however, because they will provide scientific and technical knowledge about psychomotor activity, as well as deepening the understanding of the role of sport and athletics in the United States. This background in physical education will contribute directly to career development of the sport performer and the communication specialist.

Organizations of interest to performers and sports communication persons are listed in Appendix D.

CONCEPTS TO BE GAINED FROM THIS CHAPTER

When you have mastered the material in this chapter, you will be able to demonstrate comprehension of these concepts:

1. While even a short career as a professional sport performer is probably unrealistic for most, college preparation in both business and physical education will prove beneficial for those who do succeed.
2. A career as a specialist in sports communication is or is not appropriate for you, based upon your understanding of the duties, probable future employment opportunities, and desirable educational preparation.

PERFORMING

Many persons attempt, but few succeed, in earning a living as a *professional athlete.* Even though television revenues have enabled professional tennis circuits, soccer leagues, golf tours, football conferences, etc., to expand dramatically in the past 15 years, the odds of making the team or group are very slim. It is estimated that less than 1 percent of the college male basketball players succeed in playing as a professional. Opportunities for women are even less promising, as only bowling, tennis, and golf are viable professional options available at this time.

Male professional athletes are well publicized and, in most cases, well paid. For example, the 1980 average NFL player salary was approximately $78,700, the highest being Walter Payton's $475,000. On the average, baseball players earned $150,000 in 1980, and NBA players, $180,000.

Because their skills are on constant display, most spend a great deal of time and effort on physical conditioning and psychomotor development. Unfortunately, the average professional career in basketball, football, ice hockey, and soccer is much shorter than is generally realized, probably being less than four years if all the athletes who begin each season are counted.

It is realistic to view a career as a professional athlete as a temporary one, while he or she is preparing for a more permanent career related to sport performance such as coaching, officiating, or teaching. Careers aided by a reputation gained through playing include owning or managing a sporting goods store, becoming a player's agent, or becoming a sales representative for a major sporting goods dealer. Some professional athletes leave sports completely when their playing career is over and use their contacts to gain a foothold in insurance, real estate, personnel management, or some other aspect of business.

Because of the comparatively large sums of money received by professional athletes, competent financial advice is essential. Usually, this is done by an agent—a person hired to represent the athlete. The agent, who generally receives 10 percent of the amount involved, is capable of negotiating the most advantageous contract for his or her client. This is in itself a sport-related career, most often achieved after receiving a law, business, or CPA degree.

Desirable educational preparation for a professional athletic career is primarily in business. Courses in business law, contracts, investments, and taxation are valuable, because they will give a basic background in understanding what should be considered before signing a contract. Certain courses in physical education (anatomy, physiology, biomechanics, sport psychology, coaching methods in your sport, and exercise physiology) will also be beneficial. Regardless of your college degree—whether in business or physical education—a completed degree is extremely valuable, as most players eventually enter some phase of business or a professional career.

Despite the public stereotype, *sports officials* are intelligent, well-trained, and competent persons with an encyclopedic knowledge of their sport. Opportunities for part-time work are more numerous, due primarily to the tremendous rise in female sport contests. In addition, there are opportunities to officiate in the minor leagues (basketball, baseball, football) and/or in the growing age-group sports.

Salaries, as shown in Table 15.1 are sufficient in some sports to permit a few persons to officiate full-time, at least during the season of competition. For most, however, officiating is a part-time vocation.

Preparation for officiating involves less schooling and more work of an apprenticeship type. There are baseball officiating schools, run by former major league officials. Officials in other sports must gain their education by officiating at various levels, however—and this preparation is normally completed by taking written and/or practical examinations, given by state and national organizations.

Officiating, whether done on a full- or part-time basis, is excellent preparation for those persons who will become coaches and/or physical education teachers. It is a source of income, but, more important, it aids in understanding the game, which in turn normally results in better coaching and/or teaching.

SPORTS COMMUNICATION

According to Holman (1979, p. 3), sports communication includes the print and broadcast media, plus public relations and sport promotion.

> It is a growing field of professionals who write, edit, design, manage, sell, and distribute sports sections of newspapers and magazines. In broadcasting they are the people before the cameras and microphones, and those behind the scene who are rarely seen or heard. Sports public relations and promotion persons are the middle men and women who bridge communications between sports and the consuming public.

TABLE 15.1. SALARIES OF SPORTS OFFICIALS

SPORT	STARTING WAGE	TOP WAGE
Football	$ 355/game	$ 800/game
Soccer	130/game	160/game
Tennis	12/match	30/match
Baseball	17,500/season	60,000/season
Hockey	25,000/season	60,000/season
Basketball	20,000/season	45,000/season

Source: Embattled officials explain their side, *Newsday Syndication*, Sept. 4, 1980.

Lambert (1979) reports that in 1975 there were over 11,605 job opportunities in radio, TV, or sports writing, divided as follows: 8,185 commercial and educational radio stations, 1,015 commercial and educational TV stations, 639 general and specialized magazines devoted entirely or partly to sports, and 1,766 daily newspapers. Add to these the number of colleges and professional teams who have sports information directors and promotions directors, and the artists who illustrate sport articles and books. Truly, opportunities in sport communication are available.

Sportswriters are found most often on the staffs of newspapers, as virtually every such publication has a separate section devoted to the topic. There are almost always several reporters assigned to the local sports beat; for example, Holman (1979, p. 6) reports that the sports staff of one large-city newspaper included 38 writers, editors, photographers, and editorial assistants. Stories written by these people are supplemented by material written by reporters all around the world and sent by wire to local papers.

Sport periodicals, of which *The Sporting News* and *Sports Illustrated* are the most prominent, abound in the United States. Numerous specialized publications appeal to special-interest groups; examples are *Field and Stream, Pro Football Weekly,* and *Hot Rodding*.

Sportswriters may be freelance (working independently, they sell their work to any source that will buy it) or employed by a particular periodical. In the latter case, writers are more apt to cover a variety of sports.

Salaries of sportswriters tend to be low to moderate. Those sportswriters with a regional or national reputation and/or who have written books or articles for national publications will obviously have higher incomes.

A college journalism degree is the preferred educational background for a sportswriter, but this should be supplemented by physical education activity courses as well as courses in coaching methods in various sports, organization and administration of physical education, principles of physical education, sport sociology, and sport psychology. An internship with the sports information office of your college would be highly desirable.

Broadcasters, either TV or radio, are very much in evidence. From faceless names in the studios to Bryant Gumbel or Howard Cosell, these persons are heard on every radio station and seen on every TV channel. Holman (1979, p. 6) reports that sport coverage occupies the second largest block of time on radio and TV stations, with the Super Bowl annually capturing the largest number of viewers for a single event. Cable TV will permit even more coverage of sport events in the future, thus providing sports addicts with an even greater selection.

Desirable educational preparation for broadcasters is the same as for print media specialists—a college degree in journalism or mass communications, with courses in physical education, an internship, and work experience. Gaining "on-the-air" experience is difficult, but certainly possible.

A rapidly expanding segment of the sport communications field is sport public relations and sport promotions. Income to keep sport programs going depends upon the paying fans—and the public relations/promotions persons must attract them by whatever means feasible.

A *sports information director* obtains media coverage for all aspects of the operation, issues publicity releases, and arranges for player interviews. Promotion is sometimes a separate function, but in large organizations a *promotions director* is responsible for attracting spectators and/or new members. The promotion aspect is achieved by making speeches, showing films, staging contests, and offering special promotional packages. A fund-raiser is sometimes employed by college athletic departments, but, in most cases, this function is combined with the promotions director's duties.

Both the sports information director and the promotions director work tremendously long hours during peak seasons. Unfortunately, the salary is only minimal and perhaps unequal to the responsibility.

Educational preparation includes college training in journalism, communications, and advertising plus extensive on-the-job training. Knowledge of the sport is desirable, but not essential; the principles of promotional work are the same, regardless of the product. Most public relations directors have a newspaper, radio, or TV background.

Although the opportunities are very limited, there are persons who specialize in *sports photography, painting,* or *illustrating.* While it is unlikely that there will ever be a large number of jobs available, persons with artistic ability and training may develop their own sports-related career.

Student Activity

This chapter has outlined different jobs in the performance and sports communication categories. Select the one that most interests you and submit a written report containing as much of the following material as possible:

1. Observation of the actual situation
2. Interview with someone who is now working (or has worked) in that area
3. Written information obtained from the employer or library
4. Interview with a college student who is preparing for this job.

Statements for Class Discussion

1. Realistically, my chances of becoming a professional performer are (are not) great because _____.
2. Sportswriters who are not ex-athletes just cannot get the "feel" for the game.
3. Since physical education majors tend to be leaders and enjoy performing before an audience, being a sportscaster would be easy.

Bibliography

GENERAL

Case, R. L. 1980. *Coach and the media.* Privately printed. Available from the author, Box 8104, Huntington, W. Va.

Eastman Kodak Co. 1981. *The how-to book for coaches, sports information directors and motion picture/still sports photographers.* Rochester, N.Y.: Eastman Kodak Co.

Holman, B. 1979. *Sports and mass communication.* Lexington, Mass.: Ginn and Co.

Hutter, D., *et al*. 1978. Sport and communication: An interdisciplinary curriculum. *JOPERD* 49 (January): 63.

BROADCASTING

Deford, F. 1973. It's not the game. *Sports Illustrated* 38 (April 9): 117.
Delnagro, M. 1981. Sporting a whole lot of sport. *Sports Illustrated* 52 (April 20): 76.
Fimrite, R. 1975. Lucky devil, he found heaven. *Sports Illustrated* 42 (May 12): 32-41.
Johnson, W. O. 1980. At last, all action and no talk. *Sports Illustrated* 47 (November 10): 80.
Lambert, C. 1979. Sports Communication. In Considine, W. J. *Alternative professional preparation in physical education*. Reston, Va.: AAHPERD, pp. 85-92.
Olsen, J. 1973. Virtue is its own reward. *Sports Illustrated* 38 (January 22): 64-74.

OFFICIATING

Treadwell, S. 1981. Rerun redesigns his act. *Sports Illustrated* 48 (April 20): 78-81.

PERFORMING

Drum, B. 1977. Step right up and take a whirl. *Sports Illustrated* 44 (November 11): 38-41.
O'Brien, J. 1978. Eastern league offers hope for NBA castoffs. *Sporting News* (March 18): 15.

SPORTSWRITING

Goldstein, M. 1978. Spring training was a girl's best friend. *Sporting News* (March 18): 14.
Holman, B. 1979. *Sports and mass communication*. Lexington, Mass.: Ginn and Co. See Chap. 2 (Fundamentals of sports writing) and Chap. 8 (Special problems in sports communication).

COMMITMENT

chapter 16

Physical Educator: A Career Choice

INTRODUCTION

When you began to read this text, you were fairly certain that you wanted to pursue a career in physical education. Your ideas were based mostly upon high school experiences and what you thought physical educators' jobs involved. We have attempted to expand your perception by discussing a number of concepts and careers in physical education. In this final chapter, you are asked to make decisions about continuing in physical education and sport. As mentioned earlier, this chapter will help you assess your attitude toward physical education; these assessments will be partial criteria for judgment.

A MAJOR DECISION

You have almost finished your study of this text. By now one of these statements will best represent your view.

1. I have decided to continue in physical education, either as a major or minor or to earn one of the various certificates available at my college.
2. I have decided, at least for the present, that physical education does not provide a career interest for me.

The basic points in the remainder of this chapter will apply to you, regardless of which statement you select. The details (e.g., names of organization, periodicals) are written for those who continue in physical education; for those who choose otherwise, however, the seven major points and the listing of minors apply equally.

ACTIONS LEADING TO A SUCCESSFUL CAREER

At this point you may have decided upon a career choice. In the following section are a number of things usually done by professionally minded persons. The more of these you do, the greater your obvious interest in a particular field.

Complete Courses and Achieve Above-Average Grades. For years, both students and teachers have asserted that grades receive undue importance and may not be the best indicators of what a person has gained from a class. Yet the GPA is the most important factor influencing a prospective employer—and it simply cannot be overlooked. Requirements for a particular major or certificate must be met; while you will have to achieve a certain minimum GPA to graduate (usually 2.0 for all courses taken), it should be obvious that the higher the average, the better.

Participate in Intramurals and Athletics. In physical education we claim to influence favorably the physical, social, and emotional life of the individual; intramural and athletic experiences are designed to do this. Prospective employers are favorably impressed by physical educators who participate in such activities. If we claim that they are beneficial to others, we certainly should participate ourselves. You may offer the excuse that you are too unskilled to play on a school team. A physical educator has two reasons for participating in intramurals—enjoyment (which usually comes from improved skill) and learning how these experiences affect others.

Obtain Experience. Some schools offer internship or practicum courses in which a student can gain experience and college credit for working in a real situation. In our discipline, such a course may involve helping in an elementary school physical education program (parochial schools especially need help), coaching athletics in elementary or junior high schools, working in the physical education program of the YMCA or Boys' Clubs, working in the summer as a playground director in a recreation program, working as an aide in the physical therapy department of a hospital, giving dance or swim lessons at a private sport/dance center, helping children in a day-care center, or working with the handicapped. The opportunities are endless! Sometimes these experiences can be more valuable than classroom credits. The most important thing is that these experiences are an indication of great interest in your work.

Join Professional Groups. The great majority of those persons who consider themselves professionals realize that their education includes more than classroom experience. Thus, professional organizations have been organized for virtually every interest group imaginable. Indeed, one of the common complaints of professionals is that they find it difficult to keep up with meetings and publications of the groups to which they belong, much less to broaden their knowledge by joining any new groups. Physical education is similar to other disciplines; there are at least a dozen special-interest groups. You can benefit greatly by at least reading their publications and knowing their purposes, types of organizational structure, and membership requirements. A listing at the end of the chapter indicates addresses for further information.

AAHPERD. The American Alliance for Health, Physical Education, Recreation, and Dance is a national organization that brings together administrators, teachers, and leaders in these related fields and is the largest of the various physical education groups. It was originally founded in 1885 by persons concerned with physical training. The primary purpose of AAHPERD is to strengthen and to improve school and community programs in health education, recreation, outdoor education, physical education, and professional preparation.

Organizationally, AAHPERD is structured according to geography and by interest groups. The nation is divided into six districts, with each district composed of several states. Each state has a separate association, with annual conventions at the state, district, and national levels. Associations of special interest are organized on the national level to focus attention on various aspects of our discipline. These seven associations are:

1. AALR (American Association for Leisure and Recreation)
2. ARAPCS (Association for Research, Administration, Professional Councils and Societies)
3. AAHE (American Association for Health Education)
4. ASCSA (American School and Community Safety Association)
5. NDA (National Dance Association)
6. NAGWS (National Association for Girls' and Women's Sports)
7. NASPE (National Association for Sports and Physical Education).

Like most organizations, AAHPERD has a national headquarters (Reston, VA), several publications, many committees, and self-government by an Alliance Assembly and a Board of Governors.

Membership (currently over 50,000, including more than 10,000 students) is open to all who are professionally engaged in any of the areas mentioned above. Student members are entitled to receive nine issues of *JOPERD* each year, plus fringe benefits. AAHPERD has made special efforts to enlist student support, as evidenced by:

1. Offering special bonus memberships (two years for the price of one) to graduating college seniors
2. Distributing special packets to seniors graduating with a teaching degree
3. Holding special meetings in each of the districts to train student leaders
4. Distributing materials (pamphlets, etc.) to students
5. Securing an official place in the AAHPERD structure for a council with student leaders and an all-expense-paid meeting of these officers
6. Sponsoring meetings for students at state, district, and national conventions.

Major's clubs. For many years, AAHPERD has encouraged colleges and universities to sponsor local clubs composed of major and minor students in the HPERD areas. At present there are over 200 such chartered groups. Each club is free to set its own rules and to decide its own activities. Most clubs are coeducational. As with many groups, the quality of student leadership varies from year to year, with a consequent variation in effectiveness. A major's club can add tremendously to your knowledge and professional competence. While some student clubs require members to join AAHPERD, encouragement, rather than coercion, is the usual procedure.

Professional organizations. These organizations are composed of selected groups of persons who are involved as students or professionals in á particular area. Phi Epsilon Kappa (PEK) and Delta Psi Kappa (DPK) are the professional fraternity and sorority for physical educators. These are sometimes called honorary fraternities. Most members are students, although alumni chapters and alumni membership are encouraged. The purposes of PEK and DPK are similar—to encourage greater professional competence through service with other persons who have similar interests.

PEK has 65 chapters located in various colleges and universities, while DPK has over 40 chapters. Chapters are organized according to the dictates of the national constitutions, which prescribe the officers and duties of each, the membership requirements, and the ritual. By definition, the professional fraternity exists for the professional benefit of its members. This means that various service projects (conducting sports clinics, sponsoring touring sporting groups, attending conventions, and learning about new teaching methods) are its primary activities. Social purposes are secondary to these activities. Each of these groups has a national publication: *The Physical Educator* (PEK) and *The Foil* (DPK). The chief difference between professional fraternities and major's clubs is that prospective fraternity members are selected by the active members. Merely majoring in physical education does not ensure membership.

State physical education groups. As indicated earlier, AAHPERD has organized itself on a geographic basis, and thus each state has its own Association of Health, Physical Education, Recreation, and Dance. The great majority of AAHPERD members are much more active in state affairs than they are at the district or national level. Each state has an annual AAHPERD Convention, usually located close enough to schools to allow physical education students to attend as a group. Student memberships in the state associations are available. Because it is a part of AAHPERD, the purposes are primarily the same—but with state-wide rather than national focus.

Attend Conventions and Meetings. Each state has meetings that involve physical educators. The most publicized of these are the annual meetings of teachers, but physical educators with interests other than teaching will find opportunities open to them as well. These meetings are rotated on a geographical basis from year to year. It is probable that at least one national convention will be held reasonably close to you in the four or five years of your training. This is your chance to gain knowledge and competence and to meet physical education leaders. The cost of attending meetings varies; almost all have a registration fee, and most require membership in the Alliance. Remember that one characteristic of a professional is to seek further training at his or her own expense if there is no other way.

Numerous special-interest meetings are held each year in every state. High school athletic coaches, intramural directors, teachers in inner-city schools, sport psychologists, athletic trainers, health scientists, swimming pool operators, park and recreation workers—all these groups meet occasionally. Contact your local HPERD chairperson or the physical education consultant in your state Department of Education for information on interest groups.

Purchase Books and Subscribe to Periodicals. Why not begin your professional library the economical way with student subscriptions? If you become a member of AAHPERD, your membership includes a subscription to *JOPERD*; if you join Phi Epsilon Kappa, you will receive *The Physical Educator*; Delta Psi Kappa members receive *The Foil*. Other periodicals that have great appeal and application (and sometimes student subscription rates) are *Sports Illustrated, Athletic Journal, Scholastic Coach, Psychology Today,* and *Women Sports.*

Observe and Talk With Persons in the Field. Your professors and friends are two sources of information, but perhaps the person to offer the best information is someone working in exactly the position to which you aspire.

MINORS

A basic fact is that there are usually several competent physical educators competing for each job. How can you make certain that you are given serious consideration? First, earn good grades. Second, be able to indicate to a prospective employer that you are attempting to be a professional. Join groups, attend meetings, build a library; in short, do those things discussed earlier. But there is one other step you can take to improve your attractiveness to potential employers, and that is to select a minor with care. In most schools, students have some elective hours required for graduation. Rather than take these in random fashion, why not take them in one or two disciplines?

It is impossible to develop a list of desirable minors, because the laws of supply and demand change yearly. For the latest information, consult your placement office or counseling center. For a start, however, consider this listing of minors, which is especially suitable for educators who do not plan to teach.

Psychology (motor-learning specialists)
Social Work (agency workers)
Sociology (sport sociology specialists)
Biology (exercise physiology specialists)
Computer Science (laboratory research specialists)
Chemistry (exercise physiology specialists)
Physics (motor development specialists)

A last word: selection of a minor should be on the basis of your interests and capabilities. Even if there is a surplus of persons in your field of choice, it does not mean that you should avoid that career; a well-prepared and competent professional will always succeed in his/her chosen field.

SOURCES FOR PROFESSIONAL GROWTH

Professional Groups

American Alliance for Health, Physical Education, Recreation, and Dance (AAHPERD). 1900 Association Dr., Reston, VA 22091. Ask for information about student memberships, major's clubs, and the address of your state's HPERD group.

Subgroups of AAHPERD
National Association for Girls' and Women's Sports (NAGWS)
National Association for Sports and Physical Education (NASPE)
National Dance Association (NDA)
Student Action Council of the Association for Research, Administration, Professional Councils and Societies (SAC)
All these subgroups can be contacted through AAHPERD, 1900 Association Dr., Reston, VA 22091.

Delta Psi Kappa fraternity. Business Office, c/o Mrs. John W. Schroll, Rt. 1, Box 125, Winneconne, WI 54986. Ask for the name of the nearest chapter or about the possibility of beginning a local chapter.

Phi Epsilon Kappa fraternity. Business Office, 9030 Log Run Dr. N., Indianapolis, IN 46234. Ask for the name of the nearest chapter or about the possibility of beginning a local chapter.

Professional Journals

Athletic Journal, 1719 Howard St., Evanston, IL 60202
Coach and Athlete, 1421 Mayson St. NE, Atlanta, GA 30324
Scholastic Coach, 50 W. 44th St., New York, NY 10036
Sports Illustrated, 541 N. Fairbanks Ct., Chicago, IL 60611
Women's Sports, Box 121, Mount Morris, IL 61054

Catalogs of Professional Literature

AAHPERD (address above)
Athletic Institute, 200 Castlewood Rd., North Palm Beach, FL 33408

Student Activity

As you complete this text, it is logical that you will make a decision about your future in physical education. Once this is done, you should begin to plan for the future; the assignment below will aid you.

Write an essay following *one* of the two positions outlined below. Submit this paper to your instructor, who may wish to place it in your permanent file; it will be interesting to compare your accomplishments at graduation with the plans set forth in this essay!

1. You have decided to remain in the discipline of physical education; indicate that this is a rational and planned decision by submitting an essay that includes this information:
    a. Whether you will major, minor, or earn one of the certificates
    b. A listing of those courses that you have yet to take to earn the degree or certificate that you seek
    c. A discussion of specific professional experiences that you honestly believe you will participate in before graduation. These might include: (1) intramural and athletic experiences, (2) work experiences, (3) professional groups that you will join, (4) professional meetings, conferences, and conventions (with locations and dates, if

possible) that you plan to attend, (5) professional publications that you will subscribe to, and (6) names of physical educators whom you might observe and talk to from time to time.

2. You have decided that, at least for the near future, the discipline of physical education does not provide a career interest for you. Indicate that you have gained some knowledge about our field by submitting an essay that discusses:

    a. How the physical education experiences (classes, intramurals, and/or athletics) taken have helped you physically, socially, and/or emotionally
    b. How physical education experiences you might participate in while in college will help now or in the future.

This project asks you to submit an essay on your feelings toward physical education. This is not a "busywork" assignment, because you will be affected throughout life by physical education. Presently, you are probably in a college situation that offers or even requires physical education courses. These probably should be selected for the benefit you can derive both now and in later life. You should know the objectives of our discipline (Chapters 5-10). Chapters 6-10 have indicated some of the facts and concepts related to biological development, psychomotor learning, personal expression, mechanical forces, and social, political, and economic aspects of sport. These are all directly related to the present and the future. It is logical to expect that knowledge of many of these facts and concepts might enrich your life. Wise use of leisure time is, according to some, the greatest challenge facing Americans today. We hope you have been helped in meeting this challenge.

Bibliography

AAHPERD. 1968. Major day: A PEM club project. *JOPERD* 39 (October): 101.

——. 1971. What ever happened to the PEMM clubs? *JOPERD* 42 (October): 6.

——. 1973. North Carolina State student major conventions. *JOPERD* 44 (March): 57.

Bucher, C. A. 1975. Change and challenge. *JOPERD* 46 (November-December): 55-56.

Calhoune, L. 1971. Sophomores launch elementary school physical education program. *JOPERD* 42 (February): 44.

Clendennen, W. R. 1973. Career conference for future physical educators. *JOPERD* 43 (January): 74-75.

Cody, C. 1972. Some thoughts about professional preparation. *The Physical Educator* 29 (December): 193.

Colgate, T. P. 1969. Your professional associations. *The Physical Educator* 26 (May): 79.

Crisafulli, R., *et al.* 1973. What professional involvement really means. *JOPERD* 44 (January): 69.

Eveits, C. 1972. Firsthand experiences for future physical educators. *JOPERD* 43 (October): 72.

Finn, P. 1976. Career education and P.E. *JOPERD* 47 (January): 29-30.

Louck, D. H. 1970. An educational device for developing the well-rounded physical education major. *The Physical Educator* 27 (December): 147.

Neal, J. M. 1970. Student involvement in the administration of sports programs. *JOPERD* 41 (June): 57.

Rothstein, A. 1973. Involving undergraduates in research. *JOPERD* 44 (March): 71.

Taylor, M., and Lewis, P. 1975. Every student a teacher. *JOPERD* 46 (March): 47.
Teitelbaum, B. R. 1973. A friend from Lehman. *JOPERD* 44 (January): 24-26.

APPENDIX
ORGANIZATIONS OF INTEREST TO PHYSICAL EDUCATORS

Appendix A

Organizations of Interest to Teachers and Coaches

Archery

National Field Archery Association, Rt. 2, Box 514, Redlands, CA 92373

Baseball

American Association of College Baseball Coaches, 123 Assembly Hall, Champaign, IL 62246
United States Baseball Federation, Greenville College, Greenville, IL 62246

Basketball

National Association of Basketball Coaches of the United States, P.O. Box 307, Branford, CT 06405

Boating and Canoeing

National Boating Federation, 629 Waverly Lane, Bryn Athyn, PA 19009
Scholastic Rowing Association, c/o Msgr. Glendon E. Robertson, Diocese of Camden, P.O. Box 709, Camden, NJ 08101
American Canoe Association, 4260 E. Evans Ave., Denver, CO 80222
United States Canoe Association, 606 Ross St., Middletown, OH 45042

Appendix material adapted from AAHPERD, *Weaving career education into physical education and sport* (Reston, Va.: AAHPERD, 1980).

Bowling and Billiards

American Bowling Congress (and American Junior Bowling Congress), 5301 S. 76th St., Greendale, WI 53129

Billiard Congress of America, 717 N. Michigan Ave., Chicago, IL 60611

National Duck Pin Bowling Congress, 711 14th St., N.W., Washington, DC 20005

Curling

United States Curling Association, c/o L. T. Kreutzig, 606 Highway 14 North, Harvard, IL 60033

United States Women's Curling Association, c/o Mrs. Karl J. Rustman, 1201 Somerset Dr., Glenview, IL 60025

Cycling

United States Cycling Federation, P.O. Box 699, Wall Street Station, New York, NY 10005

Dance

American Dance Guild, 1619 Broadway, Rm. 603, New York, NY 10019

Dance Educators of America, Box 470, Caldwell, NJ 07006

Dance Notation Bureau, 19 Union Square W., New York, NY 10003

National Dance Association, c/o AAHPERD, 1900 Association Dr., Reston, VA 22091

Fencing

National Fencing Coaches Association of America, Dept. of Physical Education, Baruch College, 17 Lexington Ave., New York, NY 10010

Fishing

American Casting Association, c/o William Burke, Picnic Hill, Jackson, KY 41339

Association of Surf Angling Clubs, 246 Dickinson St., Philadelphia, PA 19147

Football

National Football Foundation and Hall of Fame, 201 E. 42nd St., Suite 1506, New York, NY 10017

Pop Warner Junior League Football, 1315 Walnut St., Suite 606, Philadelphia, PA 19107

American Football Coaches Association, Box 8705, Durham, NC 27707

Golf

Professional Golfers' Association of America, Box 12458, Lake Park, FL 33403

United States Golf Association, Golf House, Far Hills, NJ 07931

Platform Tennis and Table Tennis

American Platform Tennis Association, c/o Fox Meadow Tennis Club, Wayside Lane, Scarsdale, NY 10583

United States Table Tennis Association, 1031 Jackson St., St. Charles, MO 63301

SCUBA Diving

Institute of Diving (SCUBA), City Marina, Suite 4, P.O. Box 876, Panama City, FL 32401

National Association of Underwater Instructors, P.O. Box 630, Colton, CA 92324

Professional Association of Diving Instructors, 2164 N. Bush St., Santa Ana, CA 92706

SCUBA Schools International, 1449 Riverside Dr., Fort Collins, CO 80524

Shooting

National Rifle Association of America, 1600 Rhode Island Ave., N.W., Washington, DC 20036

National Shooting Sports Foundation, 1075 Post Rd., Riverside, CT 06878

Shooters Club of America, 591 Camino De La Reina, Suite 200, San Diego, CA 92108

Skating

U.S. Figure Skating Association, 575 Boylston St., Boston, MA 02166

U.S. International Skating Association, 1166 Sherren St., W., St. Paul, MN 55113

Skiing

American Ski Association, P.O. Box 4479, Overland Park, KS 66204

American Ski Teachers Association of Natur Teknik, Camelback Ski Area, Tannersville, PA 18372

National Ski Patrol System, 2901 Sheridan Blvd., Denver, CO 80214

Professional Ski Instructors of America, 1726 Champa, Denver, CO 80202

Softball

Amateur Softball Association, 2801 N.E. 50th St., P.O. Box 11437, Oklahoma City, OK 73111

Squash

United States Squash Racquets Association, 211 Ford Rd., Bala Cynwyd, PA 19004

Swimming

American Swimming Coaches Association, One Hall of Fame Dr., Fort Lauderdale, FL 33316

College Swimming Coaches Association of America, 111 Cooke Hall, University of Minnesota, Minneapolis, MN 55455

Council for National Cooperation in Aquatics, PO Box 1574, Manassas, VA 22110

Tennis

National Tennis Foundation, 51 E. 42nd St., New York, NY 10017

United States Professional Tennis Association, 6701 Highway 58, Harrison, TN 37341

United States Tennis Association, 51 E. 42nd St., New York, NY 10017

Track and Jogging

National Jogging Association, 919 18th St., N.W., Washington, DC 20006

United States Track and Field Federation, 30 N. Norton Ave., Tucson, AZ 85719

United States Track Coaches Association, 1705 Evanston, Kalamazoo, MI 49008

Water Skiing

American Water Ski Association, S.R. 542 and Carl Floyd Rd., Winter Haven, FL 33880

Wrestling

National Wrestling Coaches Association, c/o Athletic Dept., University of Utah, Salt Lake City, UT 84112

United States Amateur Wrestling Foundation, c/o John Dustin, Wrestling Division, Amateur Athletic Union, 3400 W. 6th St., Indianapolis, IN 46268

Appendix B
Organizations of Interest to Health-Related Specialists

Fitness

American Association of Fitness Directors in Business and Industry, c/o PCPFS, Rm. 3030, 400 Sixth St., S.W., Washington, DC 20201

American Board of Fitness Instructors, 77 W. Washington St., (Suite 1708), Chicago, IL 60602

National Industrial Recreation Association, 20 N. Wacker Dr., Chicago, IL 60606

YMCA, 110 N. Wacker Dr., Chicago, IL 60606

YWCA, 600 Lexington Ave., New York, NY 10022

Sports Medicine

American College of Sports Medicine, 1440 Monroe St., Madison, WI 53706

American Physiological Society (Education Office), 9650 Rockville Pike, Bethesda, MD 20014

National Athletic Trainers' Association, 112 S. Pitt St. (P.O. Drawer 1865), Greenville, NC 27834

Rehabilitation

American Corrective Therapy Association, 6622 Spring Hollow, San Antonio, TX 78249

American Dance Therapy Association, 1821 LaCoronilla Dr., Santa Barbara, CA 93109

American Physical Therapy Association, 1156 15th St., N.W., Washington, DC 20005

Dance Therapy Association, Suite 230, 2000 Century Plaza, Columbia, MO 21044

National Therapeutic Recreation Association, 1601 N. Kent St., Arlington, VA 22209

Adapted Physical Education

American Blind Bowling Association, 150 N. Bellaire Ave., Louisville, KY 40206

Blind Outdoor Leisure Development, 533 E. Main St., Aspen, CO 81611

Consultant, Programs for the Handicapped, AAHPERD, 1900 Association Dr., Reston, VA 22091

International Committee of the Silent Sports, Gallaudet College, Washington, DC 20002

National Handicapped Sports and Recreation Association, 4105 E. Florida Ave., 3rd fl., Denver, CO 80222

National Wheelchair Athletic Association, 40-24 62nd St., Woodside, NY 11377

National Wheelchair Basketball Association, 110 Seaton Bldg., University of Kentucky, Lexington, KY 40506

North American Biking for the Handicapped Association, c/o Leonard Warner, P.O. Box 100, Ashburn, VA 22011

Physical Education and Recreation Office, Division of Professional Preparation, Bureau of Education for the Handicapped, 7th and D Sts., Washington, DC 20202

Special Olympics, 1701 D St., N.W., Suite 203, Washington, DC 20006

United States Deaf Skiers Association, 159 Davis Ave., Hackensack, NJ 07601

Appendix C
Organizations of Interest to Sales and Management Persons

Archery

Archery Lane Operators Association, 2151 N. Hamline Ave., Suite 201, St. Paul, MN 55113

Archery Manufacturers Organizations, 200 Castlewood Rd., North Palm Beach, FL 33408

Bicycles and Motorcycles

American Association of Bicycle Importers, 200 Fifth Ave., New York, NY 10010

Bicycle Manufacturers Association, 1101 15th St., N.W., Washington, DC 20005

Bicycle Wholesale Distributors Association, Box 594, 95 E. Valley Stream Blvd., Valley Stream, NY 11580

Cycle Parts and Accessories Association, 122 E. 42nd St., New York, NY 10017

National Bicycle Dealers Association, 29023 Euclid Ave., Wickliffe, OH 44092

Books

Association of American Publishers, One Park Ave., New York, NY 10016

Bowling

Bowling Proprietors Association of America, P.O. Box 5802, Arlington, TX 76011

Camping

American Camping Association, Bradford Woods, Martinsville, IN 46151

Dance

Association of American Dance Companies, 162 W. 56th St., New York, NY 10019

Choreographers Theater, 25 W. 19th St., New York, NY 10011

Managers of Larger Dance Companies of North America, c/o Gerald Ketelaar, Cleveland Ballet, 1375 Euclid Ave., Suite 330, Cleveland, OH 44115

Fishing

American Fishing Tackle Manufacturers Association, 20 N. Wacker Dr., Chicago, IL 60606

Tackle Representatives Association International, 20 N. Wacker Dr., Suite 1930, Chicago, IL 60606

Golf

Golf Ball Manufacturers Association, 200 Castlewood Rd., North Palm Beach, FL 33408

Golf Course Builders of America, 725 15th St., N.W., Suite 700, Washington, DC 20005

Golf Course Superintendents Association of America, 1617 St. Andrews Dr., Lawrence, KS 66044

Manufacturing Jewelers Golf Association, c/o Roland and Whytock Co., Inc., 75 Oxford St., Providence, RI 02905

National Association of Golf Ball Manufacturers, 200 Castlewood Rd., North Palm Beach, FL 33408

National Golf Foundation, 200 Castlewood Rd., North Palm Beach, FL 33408

Professional Groups

National Sporting Goods Association, 717 N. Michigan Ave., Chicago, IL 60611

Sporting Goods Agent's Association, P.O. Box A, Morton Grove, IL 60053

Sport Management Art and Science Society, c/o Harold VanderZwaag, Dept. of Sport Studies, Hicks Bldg., University of Massachusetts, Amherst, MA 01003

Racquetball and Handball

United States Racquetball Association, 4101 Dempster St., Skokie, IL 60076

National Court Clubs Association, 360 Park Dr., Northbrook, IL 60062

Skating, Skateboarding, and Skiing

Ice Skating Institute of America, 1000 Skokie Blvd., Wilmette, IL 60091

International Skateboard Association, 711 17th St., Suite E-7, Costa Mesa, CA 92627

National Ski Areas Association, P.O. Box 83, West Hartford, CT 06107

Roller Skating Foundation of America, 515 Madison Ave., New York, NY 10022

Roller Skating Rink Operators Association of America, 7700 A St., Lincoln, NE 68501

Ski Council of America, 600 Madison Ave., New York, NY 10022

Ski Area Suppliers Association, Box 500, North Salem, NY 10560

Swimming and Aquatics

National Aquatic Sports Camps, 8601 Riggs, Overland Park, KS 66206

National Swimming Pool Institute, 2000 K St., N.W., Washington, DC 20006

Tennis

National Indoor Tennis Association, P.O. Box 11097, Chicago, IL 60611

U.S. Paddle Tennis Association, 189 Seeley St., Brooklyn, NY 11218

Appendix D
Organizations of Interest to Performers and Sports Communication Persons

Performers

Amateur Fencers League of America, 601 Curtis St., Albany, CA 94706

Association of Professional Ball Players of America, 337 E. San Antonio Dr., Suite 203, Long Beach, CA 90807

Association of Tennis Professionals, World Trade Center, Box 58144, Dallas, TX 75258

International Volleyball Association, 1901 Ave. of the Stars, Suite 610, Los Angeles, CA 90067

Ladies Professional Golf Association, 919 Third Ave., New York, NY 10022

National Basketball Association, 645 Fifth Ave., New York, NY 10022

National Football League, 410 Park Ave., New York, NY 10022

Professional Archers Association, 4711 S. Brennan Rd., Helmock, MI 48625

Professional Bowlers Association of America, 1720 Merriman Rd., Akron, OH 44313

U.S. Soccer Federation, 350 Fifth Ave., New York, NY 10001

Women's Professional Bowlers Association, 204 W. Wacker Dr., Suite 300, Chicago, IL 60606

Officials

International Association of Approved Basketball Officials, 1620 Dual Highway E., Hagerstown, MD 21740

National Association of League Umpires and Scorers (Baseball), Box 1420, Wichita, KS 67201

National Intercollegiate Soccer Officials' Association, 131 Moffitt Blvd., Islip, NY 11751

United States Volleyball Association, P.O. Box 77065, San Francisco, CA 94107

Sports Communication Persons

American Council on Education for Journalism, 563 Essex Ct., Deerfield, IL 60015

Baseball Writers Association of America, 36 Brookfield Rd., Fort Salonga, NY 11768

Bowling Writers Association of America, c/o Chicago *Tribune* Sports, Chicago, IL 60611

Committee on Research in Dance, 35 W. 4th St., Rm. 6750, New York University, Dept. of Dance Education, New York, NY 10003

Football Writers Association of America, Box 1022, Edmondson, OK 73034

Golf Writers Association of America, 1720 Section Rd., Suite 210, Cincinnati, OH 45237

National Association of Broadcasters, 1771 N St., N.W., Washington, DC 20036

Professional Football Writers of America, c/o Baton Rouge *Morning Advocate*, 4758 Marque Dr., New Orleans, LA 70127

Society for American Baseball Research, P.O. Box 323, Cooperstown, NY 13326

Underwater Photography Instruction Association, Key Largo Diving Hdqtrs., Rt. One, Box 293, Key Largo, FL 33037

United States Basketball Writers Association, 307 N. Pennsylvania St., Indianapolis, IN 46206

U.S. Tennis Writers Association, c/o Ron Bookman, *World Tennis Magazine* 383 Madison Ave., New York, NY 10017

Index

**STUDENTS, TELL THE AUTHORS
AND THE PUBLISHER WHAT YOU THINK!**

Students are shaping the curricula, texts, and materials that have a role in determining the effectiveness of their education. Both the authors and Burgess Publishing want your opinion of this book. We want to develop better textbooks. Please tell us what you like about this book. Please tell us about improvements you think should be made. We'll be grateful. And, if you give your mailing address, WE WILL REFUND DOUBLE YOUR POSTAGE.

Your name (optional) _____

School _____ Your mailing address _____

City _____ State _____ Zip_____

Course title _____ Instructor's name _____

1. How does this book compare with other texts you have used? Check one.

   ☐ better than any other   ☐ better than most
   ☐ about the same as the rest ☐ not as good as most

2. Circle those chapters you especially liked:

   Chapters: 1 2 3 4 5 6 7 8 9 10 11 12 13 14 15 16

   Comments:

3. Circle those chapters you think could be improved:

   Chapters: 1 2 3 4 5 6 7 8 9 10 11 12 13 14 15 16

   Comments:

4. Please list any chapters that were not assigned by your instructor.

5. What additional topics did your instructor discuss that were not covered in this text?

OVER, PLEASE

6. After taking the course, are you interested in taking more courses in this field? ☐ yes ☐ no

7. Was the text helpful in your decision to pursue physical education as a career path? ☐ yes ☐ no

8. What suggestions do you have to help us improve this textbook?

9. Please give us your impressions of the text by rating the following:

	Poor		Average		Excellent
Logical organization	1	2	3	4	5
Readability of text material	1	2	3	4	5
General layout and design	1	2	3	4	5
Match with instructor's course organization	1	2	3	4	5
Illustrations that clarify the text	1	2	3	4	5
Up-to-date treatment of subject	1	2	3	4	5
Explanation of difficult concepts	1	2	3	4	5
Selection of topics in the text	1	2	3	4	5

10. Do you plan to keep the book or sell it? ☐ keep it ☐ sell it

11. General comments:

Please check here if you have any objections to being quoted in our advertising. ☐

To mail, remove this page and mail to:

WE WILL REFUND DOUBLE YOUR POSTAGE!

(We are sorry, but postal regulations make it difficult for us to use a postal return permit.)

Both the authors and the publisher thank you.

Wayne Schotanus
Physical Education Editor
Burgess Publishing Company
7108 Ohms Lane
Minneapolis, MN 55435